The
Georgian Bracket Clock
—— 1714-1830 ——

FRONTISPIECE *John Naylor. London and Nantwich. A large and very rare spring-driven astronomical calendar clock in an inverted bell-top ebonised case.* Circa *1725.*

The
Georgian Bracket Clock
——1714-1830——

Richard C. R. Barder

The Antique Collectors' Club

For Philippa, Edward and Charles.
With love.

British Library Cataloguing-in-Publication Data
A catalogue record for this book is available from the British Library.

Printed in England by
The Antique Collectors' Club Ltd., Woodbridge, Suffolk, IP12 1DS
on Consort Royal Silk from The Donside Paper Company, Aberdeen, Scotland

Contents

Foreword

This is a book which will satisfy a long-felt need and should continue to do so for a considerable time. It was commissioned to extend and complete the story of the bracket or spring clock, the early history of which is given in considerable detail in *Early English Clocks*, also published by the Antique Collectors' Club.

The earlier work covers only clocks with square or rectangular dials, ceasing at the point, *circa* 1720, where the break arch dial became popular. Dick Barder, in his introductory chapter, gives an excellent account of the state of the art by this date and of the organisation and development of the trade during the seventeenth and eighteenth centuries. This provides a good introduction for readers who do not possess the earlier book.

For the period covered by the title the author very thoroughly describes the development of cases, dials and movements, all profusely illustrated by a wide range of carefully chosen photographs showing both typical and rare examples of provincial as well as London clocks. His researches into the export market make a useful contribution to our knowledge of this often neglected aspect of the trade.

Dick Barder has acquired his deep knowledge of the subject as a result of many years of handling antique clocks. Fortunately he also has the ability to set out his knowledge in a clear and easily read form. Each new aspect of the subject is properly introduced and the ample footnotes are evidence of his sound research.

I am pleased to be associated with this book.

Tom Robinson

John Ellicott. Handsome walnut clock with unusual flyback date feature in the arch. Circa 1730. *See also Colour Plate 5.* Page 55.

John Drury. Four train musical clock. See also Colour Plate 26. Page 164.

Acknowledgements

I am very grateful to many people for their help in the preparation of this book. First I thank my wife and business partner Philippa for deciphering and word processing the manuscript, for her constant encouragement and for many constructive suggestions.

I also thank C. R. P. Allix and L. Harvey for allowing me to reprint the lucid explanation of silent pull and pull-quarter repeating work in English bracket clocks given in *Hobson's Choice*, D. M. Penny for his line drawings and H. Yorke-Davies who took nearly all the photographs attributed to Richard Barder Antiques. Considerable assistance was also received from D. Berkeley, Mrs R.W. Cameron, P. G. Dawson, the Hon. P. H. Dixon, N. Evans, Mrs M. F. Figgis, Miss G. Lee, B. Loomes, D. H. Roberts, M. P. Sampson, Mrs R. Shenton, R. H. Stenning, M. S. Turner, Lady E. White and B. P. L. M. Wright.

I thank too C. Armour, D. R. and M. A. Beney, The Trustees of the British Museum, A. Brocklehurst, M. P.W. Brown, K. Bryon, M. Camarsa, D. Davies, F. A. Evans CVO, J. L. Evans, R. Garnier, Miss S. George, C. Greenwood, R. Harwood, F. Hudson, J. G. Howard, J. Jeffery, Miss J. Knott, R. C. G. Lister, A. Little, J. Lowe, J. G. Mighell, Miss C.E. Niles, C.J. Pickford, M. and P. Oxley, R. Price, D. and S. Pullen, A. J. and R. Radcliffe, D. M. Radford, N. Raffety, P. Roberts, J. P. Rylands, J. Snellenburg, A. L. Spiller, Mrs S. Stuart, The Trustees of the Victoria and Albert Museum, A. H. Weeving, K. Wills, A Woodburn, and J.R. Ziegler. Finally, I thank my mother Lesley Barder who first stimulated my interest in antique clocks.

Introduction

Tremendous advances were made in clockmaking in Britain during the last decades of the seventeenth century. By 1714, the start of the Georgian epoch, British clockmakers were rightly acknowledged to be the best in the world. They maintained this position until well into the nineteenth century and only lost their lead because they refused to lower their standards or change their manufacturing methods to compete with the cheaper clocks that flooded into Britain from Germany and the United States of America. Inevitably their businesses declined. By the end of the nineteenth century only a tiny handful of traditional makers survived.

Many different types of clock were produced during the years of British supremacy but what is not generally realised is that the majority of the finest and most costly clocks made were not the familiar longcases but bracket clocks which, despite their name, were more often placed upon tables, chests of drawers or other suitable pieces of furniture.

The reason that bracket clocks were more expensive was that the making of springs and the fusée which maintains an even delivery of power as the spring runs down, was a lengthy and highly skilled process. Additionally, many bracket clocks had extra refinements such as quarter chiming or repeating work. They were invariably finished to a high standard and were housed in elegant and costly cases. The result was that from the very first these fine clocks were the province of the nobility and wealthier classes. It is not surprising that the leading makers reserved their best efforts for their production.

Interest in antique clocks has grown apace during the twentieth century. There is now a considerable literature. But whereas the late Stuart bracket clocks (those made during the last decades of the seventeenth century and the first few years of the eighteenth century) have been the subject of continuous and intensive study, surprisingly little attention has been paid to the many different types of bracket clock that were produced during the Georgian era, which spans the much longer period from 1714 to 1830. This is a considerable oversight. The Georgian bracket clock, with its beautifully made movement and restrained, elegant casework, so perfectly in tune with the English taste, was a prized possession during an epoch which many people today regard as having produced all that is best in art, architecture and furniture.

The study of bracket clocks of the preceding late Stuart period culminated in the publication of Dawson, Drover and Parke's *Early English Clocks*, which also encompassed early longcases and lantern clocks. In this book the study is continued by illustrating and discussing a large number of bracket clocks of the ensuing period.

Brothers Melly and Martin.
Movement. Circa *1795.*

CHAPTER ONE
Background

Domestic clocks first came into general use in Britain with the introduction of the lantern clock early in the seventeenth century. The earliest form of lantern clock had an escapement controlled by a balance wheel. By 1658 the pendulum controlled verge escapement had come into use and the first longcases had appeared. Within a year or two bracket clocks were being made.[1] By the end of the century clockmaking was a well-established trade and clockmakers were to be found in every part of the country.

The trade in London, of particular importance for reasons which will soon be apparent, was largely, though never completely, regulated by the Clockmakers' Company which was founded in 1631.

The Clockmakers' Company performed a number of functions. It provided financial help for members who fell on hard times and helped the widows of clockmakers. It ensured, or tried to ensure, that high standards of workmanship were maintained and controlled the numbers and training of apprentices taken by its members. The number of apprentices was important; only two per member were allowed at a time. The Company believed that by thus limiting the output and number of clockmakers there would be no unemployment among its members.

Apprentices were normally bound to a master for seven years at the age of fourteen. The intention was that the boy should obtain his Freedom at the age of twenty-one having learned every aspect of the trade. On becoming Free it was usual for the young clockmaker to work as a journeyman, i.e. a qualified clockmaker in the employ of an established master, for a further two years in

Obadiah Grevill. Circa 1685.

---

1 During the late seventeenth and eighteenth centuries bracket clocks were usually known as spring clocks. Tompion referred to them as such in his bills. Haggar and Miller, in *Suffolk Clocks and Clockmaking* cite Bilby Dorling's advertisement in the *Ipswich Journal* of 6th October, 1764 'that he was to be found At the sign of the Spring Clock, at Cooks Row.' There are other contemporary examples of this nomenclature. There are also contemporary Georgian references to table clocks. The origin and date of the description Bracket Clock is uncertain but may be presumed to be nineteenth century. Interestingly, Deryck Roberts, in *The Bracket Clock* cites a shipping order of 1802 in which all the bracket clocks are described as spring clocks whereas in a

London price list of 1834 the bracket clocks are described as bracket clocks. Cescinsky and Webster, in *English Domestic Clocks,* first published in 1913, note that the name Bracket Clock is used through custom. It is still the custom today. Andrew Nicholls, author of *English Bracket and Mantel Clocks* published in 1981, defined bracket clocks as follows:

'Bracket clocks are those which are spring driven and housed in wooden cases. They are normally portable and capable of being stood on a bracket mounted on the wall. A few were originally supplied with matching brackets from which they derive their name. The great majority, however, never had a bracket and simply stood on

a suitable piece of furniture... Miniature bracket clocks small enough to stand on the mantelpiece are sometimes regarded as mantel clocks. Towards the end of the 18th century, and throughout the 19th century a type of case designed specifically to stand on the mantelpiece was produced. It was made of any material other than wood. Ormolu, bronze, marble and porcelain were all unaffected by the heat from a fire and were eminently suitable.'

The writer agrees with this definition but would add that the usual custom today is to describe very small wooden-cased bracket clocks as bracket clocks if they are Georgian whereas if they are of later manufacture they are usually described as mantel clocks.

order to widen his experience before setting up as a master in his own right, though some clockmakers were content to remain as journeymen.

There are many instances of apprentices failing to take up their Freedom. Some of these young men had come from the provinces and intended setting up in business in their home towns and villages. Others were Londoners who felt there were better opportunities in the provinces. There was no point in joining the Clockmakers' Company and paying your quarterage if you did not intend to work in London. Others knew they would not rise in their profession and worked as unlicensed journeymen. Presumably they were paid less but they avoided paying quarterage. There were also young men who died or were found to be totally unsuitable for the work.

A Free master clockmaker needed, at least in theory, to be a Freeman of the City of London as well as being Free of the Clockmakers' Company before he could set up shop and put his name to clocks in London but the system was riddled with inconsistencies. In the early days before the Clockmakers' Company, clockmakers had obtained their Freedoms through other Companies and not all of them wished to join the new Company. They continued to free their apprentices in the Companies to which they already belonged. Freedom of a recognised City Company gave an almost automatic right to City Freedom. But a Company Freedom gained by serving an apprenticeship, Freedom by servitude as it was known, was only one method. Another was called Freedom by patrimony. A man who was free of a Company had the automatic right to free his son in that Company. A boy could be apprenticed to a clockmaker yet finally freed in the Grocers' Company if his father was free of the Grocers. He would then be styled Citizen and Grocer on taking up his City Freedom yet be perfectly free in every sense to set up shop as a clockmaker. Inevitably, the number of clockmakers who were not members of the Clockmakers' Company increased. In the second half of the eighteenth century the Clockmakers' Company resorted to making prominent clockmaking non-members Honorary Freemen in an attempt to gather them into the Company fold.

Clockmakers who came to London from the provinces or from abroad, or had served their apprenticeship in other Companies, had to produce proof of apprenticeship before they could become members of the Clockmakers' Company. They were then called Free Brothers and could only take apprentices through other members who were full Freemen. Technically a Free Brother could not sign his work and could rise no higher than being a journeyman in the employ of a full Freeman. But a Free Brother could become a full Freeman on payment of a fee to the Company. This was called Freedom by redemption.

A Free brother who was already Free of another Company could of course bind an apprentice directly to himself through his original Company and free him in that Company too. He could have already taken up his own City Freedom through his original Company. It also seems clear that City Freedoms were sometimes routed through a third Company. Christopher Gould, a famous late seventeenth century maker, is thought to have been apprenticed and presumably freed in the Loriners' Company. He became a Free Brother in the Clockmakers' Company in 1682 and subsequently took four apprentices through various full Freemen. In 1695 he took up his City Freedom, it is believed through the Glovers' Company. His apprentices were then taken as if he was a full Freeman of the Clockmakers', which he never was, even though he ultimately became its Beadle.

It is not surprising that clocks are often found signed by men who were not members of the Clockmakers' Company or are listed only as having been apprentices or Brothers. In many instances there is no apparent record of these makers whatsoever, though many apprenticeships and freedoms must still be buried in the records of other City Companies. Needless to say, a clock should always be judged on its own merits. Many fine examples were made by men who are unknown or little known.

There was considerable room for manoeuvre within the system.[2] The most irksome regulation for a successful maker was the restriction on the number of apprentices. Apprentices, or rather their parents, paid a premium, usually between £10 and £30, for the privilege of being taught the trade. After a year or two a promising apprentice became a useful employee who cost his master nothing except his lodging. Extra apprentices could be taken but only on payment of a sizeable fine to the Company.

Thomas Tompion, the most famous English maker, always needed a large workforce. He employed a judicious mixture of Clockmakers' Company apprentices and journeymen, who in turn were entitled to take apprentices. In addition he employed a clockmaker free of another Company, the Goldsmiths', who in turn could take useful apprentices.[3] They in time became his journeymen and continued in Tompion's employ. Their parent Company, the Goldsmiths', raised no objection. The apprenticeships were in order and the clockmaker Goldsmiths were no threat to the livelihood of the bona fide goldsmithing Goldsmiths.

Specialisation, batch production and division of labour were already common enough in seventeenth century London for Heinrich Ludolf Benhem[4], who visited England in 1687, to comment...

> ...'I must mention that in London different sorts of handicraftsmen work at a clock and those that assemble the pieces and parts that have been manufactured by others are called the actual clockmaker.'

There can be no doubt that this specialisation increased tremendously during the eighteenth and early part of the nineteenth centuries. Specialisation had its advantages. It allowed the London maker to devote all his energies to perfecting the design and appearance of his clocks while allowing him the freedom to order each component or even the entire movement from the person or firm best suited to its manufacture. In the hands of a top maker it was a system that produced exceptional results.

But what of the provinces? The student of Georgian bracket clocks cannot fail to have noticed that, whereas longcase clocks seem to have been made in every part of the country during the period 1714-1830, bracket clocks, certainly until nearly the end of the eighteenth century, almost invariably bear

2 For a fuller explanation of the system see *Early English Clocks* by Dawson, Drover and Parkes and *The Early Clockmakers of Great Britain* by B. Loomes.

3 'Who was Harry Callowe?', Guy Boney QC, *Antiquarian Horology*, Autumn 1987.

4 *Englaender Kirch und Schulen Staat.* Quoted by R.W. Symonds, *Thomas Tompion. His Life and Work.*

Nathaniel Hodges. Backplate. Circa *1690.*

5 Dawson, Drover and Parkes, *Early English Clocks,* illustrate a bracket clock by John Witherston of Hereford, *circa* 1690 which they describe as made in London and partially engraved but finished and signed 'John Witherston Hereford fecit.'

6 'The Context of Production, identification and dating of clocks by A & J Thwaites'. G.T.E. Buggins and A.J. Turner. *Antiquarian Horology,* September 1973.

the names of London makers. Even during the Regency a provincial bracket clock was a rarity. It would be reasonable to conclude that London makers possessed extra skills that were lacking in the provinces.

Nothing could be further from the truth. Enough provincially made bracket clocks, including many from the pre-1750 period, have survived for us to be sure that many provincial makers possessed the skills. Their bracket clocks are usually of good, and often of excellent, quality. The detail work is sufficiently individual for us to be sure that they were not, as is often suggested, always ordered from London and merely signed by the men who sold them in the provinces. Indeed the Georgian provincial maker, working on his own or at the most with two or three assistants, had of necessity to be more versatile and to have developed a much wider range of skills than those possessed by many of his London counterparts.

It is true to say that even well before the middle of the eighteenth century communications were good enough for a provincial maker to order components or even a complete movement, whether longcase or bracket, in the unfinished or finished state, from one of the several wholesale trade manufacturers in London; some makers undoubtedly did so,[5] but it is also true to say that it would have been logistically difficult and extremely uneconomic for a provincial maker to do anything other than make as much of his clock as possible in his own workshop. Even right at the end of the period, by which time we were becoming an industrialised nation with a widespread capacity to produce well-made mechanical artefacts, the provincial maker probably spent much more of his own time fitting and finishing his movements than his London counterpart who had always been able to call on the different skills of a vast number of easily accessible specialist tradesmen.

It is interesting to assess some of the work of the Thwaites family, who became wholesale clock manufacturers in London. A record of some 2600 jobs carried out for no less than 193 different makers was compiled from John Thwaites' day books which survive from 1780.[6] Unfortunately, the day books from the preceding twenty years are missing, but the Thwaites family production of clocks of various types between 1761 and 1830 has been estimated at more than eight thousand. It has not been possible to identify all of the 193 makers whose names have been extracted from the day books but the vast majority of those that can be identified are London men. Orders from provincial makers account for less than 150 of the total of 2600 jobs and were not necessarily all orders for bracket clocks. These 150 jobs are spread over only some twenty makers. The number is probably less, because men listed as having worked in London and the provinces and those men who might have been either the London or the provincial maker of the same name have been attributed to the provinces. These figures do not suggest much dependence on London, even allowing for the fact that bracket clocks were not sold in quantity in the provinces.

One important aspect of bracket clockmaking which would have been outside the competence of the clockmaker, whether in London or the provinces, was spring making. Springs would have been ordered from a specialist clock spring maker in London in the early days, though later there were spring makers in the major provincial industrial centres. Engraving was another specialist trade. Some provincial makers, those in rural areas far from the services of a professional engraver, had learned to engrave tolerably well but even the smallest and most remote maker would have employed a specialist engraver for an order as important as a bracket clock. In Chapter II, a bracket clock by Joseph Kirk of Harstoft is illustrated and described which bears the name of its London engraver on the back of the chapter ring, though it is abundantly clear that the movement is Kirk's own work.

Clock casemaking was obviously outside the realm of clockmaking. In London the casemaker would have been a member of the Joiners' Company. The Apprenticeship and Freedom records of the Joiners' Company still exist and it is known that some members specialised in clock casemaking even during the late Stuart period. Unfortunately, as joiners did not sign their pieces, we can identify the work of very few of them. In the provinces clock cases were made' by joiners with the necessary skills but, as relatively few orders were taken for bracket clocks, their cases would have been careful copies of London examples or even ordered from London casemakers. It is for this reason that provincial bracket clock cases are, with a very few exceptions, stylistically identical to London examples though the design details might lag a few years behind. At no time were there different schools of provincial bracket clock casemaking and clockmaking such as developed in, and were such a feature of, provincial longcases. The main reason for this was that too few provincial bracket clocks were made for provincial styles to develop.

Nathaniel Hodges. Circa *1690.*

The reasons for the small provincial demand will be examined shortly but it must be evident that the good provincial maker, having taken his order for a bracket clock, had no alternative but to turn to London, the biggest producer of bracket clocks and thus the creator of the only 'school' of bracket clockmaking, for his inspiration. There is no reason to suppose that the provincial maker was in any way out of his depth. He knew that he, his engraver and his casemaker had the requisite skills. All they needed was the design information. It is quite certain that a good and prosperous provincial maker would have long established his lines of communication. He would have visited the capital from time to time and would have bought small sundries such as hands and spandrels from London trade suppliers. We may be sure that his sharp eye also took in many other details of London practice and manufacture. Additionally, he would have had London bracket clocks brought to him for repair. And increasingly, as the eighteenth century advanced, there must have been wholesalers' pattern and price books available, not only to the clockmaker, but also to his engraver and casemaker. All in all the good provincial maker must have been perfectly familiar with London styles and methods. It will come as no surprise to find that the provincial Georgian bracket clock is usually virtually identical to its London counterpart. But here perhaps we have the origin of the oft repeated assertion that provincial bracket clocks look so like London clocks that they must all have been made in London.

Here is an interesting example that introduces what will be seen to be the most important factor underlying the scarcity of provincial examples. It is provided by Dr Claver Morris, whose diary and accounts for the years 1703-23 came to light in an old chest of drawers.[7]

'..Jan. 13 1709. To Christopher Tucker
for a repeating spring piece without any case to this clock £7.'

'..March 18 1709. I gave Thomas Parfitt for his journey he lately went for me to see my brother Prowse's spring repeating clock case. 12½d.' (Thomas Parfitt, a local craftsman, is sent to see what a bracket clock case looks like.)

'..1710. To Thos Parfitt for a shelf for my repeater.'

'..1710. To Mr. Hill by order of Mr. Wood in London for my repeating clock case of ebony 35 shillings.'

Ebony, a rare imported wood, cost more than walnut. It was probably not available to Thomas Parfitt, though ebonised pearwood would have been an effective and available substitute. But on this occasion the order for the case went to London.

The significance of the total price of £8.15s. will be apparent when it is realised that a thirty hour oak longcase clock by a small market town maker such as Samuel Roberts,[8] of Llanvair in Montgomeryshire cost between £3 and £4, less than half the price of Dr Claver Morris' timepiece bracket clock. Dr Claver Morris' clock would have cost far more had it been a striking and repeating clock instead of only striking the hours and quarters when a string was pulled.

Samuel Roberts made a total of about six hundred longcase clocks during a working life of forty-one years. But less than six of these were eight day clocks. They cost £5-£6 each. Although his clocks sold over a large area he never took a single order for a bracket clock.

It is evident that small country makers relied almost exclusively on orders for thirty hour longcase clocks. Makers in the provincial cities and larger towns made a very occasional bracket clock and made eight day longcases for the local gentry, richer farmers and wealthier merchants. Sometimes an order would be taken for a turret clock for a church or large country house. Lantern clocks were made in the provinces until quite late in the eighteenth century and there was some sale of weight driven wall and alarum clocks. But even the grandest provincial maker had a bread and butter trade in the staple thirty hour longcase clocks.

It is clear that a bracket clock costing considerably more than an eight day longcase, itself a luxury that could only be afforded by the better-off, was not likely to be made in quantity. So why are there so many London-made bracket clocks? The answer is revealed by looking at the population figures. In 1770 York had a population of 17,000, Oxford under 12,000, Bristol 40,000, Norwich 30,000, and Birmingham 30,000. But the population of London was 810,000. Quite simply there were fewer people of means in the provinces and those that had the means were the very people who would have made frequent visits to London. Bracket clocks are easily transportable. Many must have

7 Quoted by J.K. Bellchambers in *Somerset Clockmakers* by permission of Sir Charles Hobhouse.
8 *Samuel Roberts. Clockmaker. An eighteenth century craftsman in a Welsh rural Community,* W.T.R. Price and T. Alun Davies.

been purchased on visits to the capital. To sum up, it was lack of demand rather than lack of ability that accounts for the shortage of provincially signed bracket clocks.

Freedom to set up in business in a provincial city or large town was normally granted on payment of a fee and proof of having served an apprenticeship, but trading freedom might be delayed or refused if there were already several men engaged in the same trade. Joseph Knibb encountered strong opposition when he tried to set up shop in Oxford.[9] Knibb eventually went to London but there are many examples of London-trained makers setting up in the provinces in areas where there was a shortage of clockmakers.

There were no formal requirements for the maker setting up in a small town or village, save that it would be expected that he would have served an apprenticeship. Many of the smaller county makers sold their clocks on market day in small towns or large villages. As a result, clocks by the same maker will sometimes be found signed for several different places.

Clockmaking was an expanding business throughout the eighteenth and first part of the nineteenth centuries. It is not surprising that it attracted men of considerable mathematical and mechanical ability from a wide variety of backgrounds.

It was noted in the Introduction that the bracket clocks of the Stuart period had been studied in detail by Dawson, Drover and Parkes in *Early English Clocks* but a brief résumé of the salient features of some of these early clocks will be useful to those unfamiliar with bracket clocks of the period.

The first English bracket clocks were made *circa* 1660. These first generation Stuart clocks had architectural cases and movements with countwheel striking but it is the second generation clocks that started to appear *circa* 1680 that are of particular interest because they are in every sense the progenitors of the clocks of the Georgian period.

The majority of the second generation clocks had dome top wooden cases and rack striking. Occasionally, the domed top of the case to which the handle was affixed was made of pierced brass, known as a basket top. The dome top case is important because it is the first real bracket clock case style. It is neither strictly utilitarian in the sense that the very earliest purely functional cases were merely an attempt to enclose the mechanism nor, as were the architectural cases, is it a recognizable adaption of the hood of an early longcase clock.

Bracket clocks made between 1680 and 1714 are important for two further reasons. First, considerable mechanical advances were made. It may not be generally realised, but it is effectively true to say, that virtually every mechanical feature found in clocks made throughout the ensuing Georgian period was already in use in a fully developed form in bracket clocks made between 1680 and 1714. Second, it was during this period too that the methods and materials used in the construction of bracket clock cases became established and formalised. Indeed the only new material, albeit an important one, to be introduced after 1714 was mahogany, which was first imported quite early in the eighteenth century but was seldom used for clock cases until about 1750.

9 *Clockmaking in Oxfordshire*, C.F.C. Beeson.

2

1

PLATE I/1 *John Knibb, Oxford. Wood dome top bracket clock. Gilded mounts, handle and dial plate. Signed on dial plate. Minute divisions on edge of chapter ring.* Circa *1685.*

PLATE I/2 *Tulip engraved backplate of John Knibb clock. Simple back-cock, verge escapement.*

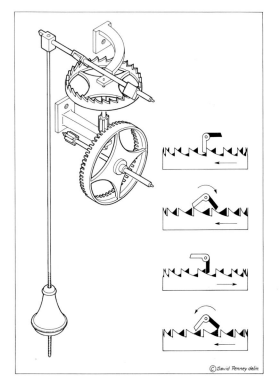

Figure (a) *Knife-edge verge escapement.*

The dome top bracket clock illustrated in Plate I/1 is typical of the 1680-85 period. The case stands about 12 inches high excluding the cast brass handle and is made of ebonised pearwood veneered onto a carcase of oak. Many cases made both before and during the Georgian period were veneered with ebony,[10] but ebonised pearwood, which gives a similar effect but was less expensive than the imported ebony, was a much used finish for black clocks. Black clocks remained popular throughout the Georgian period, probably because black contrasts well with brass dials and case mounts. Some clocks, this is an example, had gilded mounts and dials. The clock is signed in the early manner on the dial plate below the chapter ring, 'John Knibb Oxon fecit'. John Knibb was the younger of the two famous Knibb brothers. He remained in business in Oxford when Joseph moved to London in 1670. The similarity of bracket clocks made by the brothers is so marked, at least until Joseph retired to Hanslope in 1697, that it has been surmised[11] that John's clocks were made in London by Joseph and sent to Oxford for him to sell but it is more likely that the brothers worked closely together and that each used the workshop facilities and casemaker of the other as supply and demand dictated.

The dial of John Knibb's clock is clear and uncluttered. It shows only hours and minutes. The only extra feature is the Strike/Silent knob. The minute divisions are engraved on the extreme edge of the chapter ring, an early feature, but one that is sometimes seen on clocks made right up to the end of the seventeenth century. The quarter hour markers round the inside of the chapter ring are a feature that will persist until nearly the middle of the eighteenth century. They were an invaluable aid to the many people used only to one-handed lantern and thirty hour longcase clocks showing only hours and quarters. It should be remembered that lantern clocks were made until fairly late in the eighteenth century. The now neglected single handed thirty hour longcase was by far the most common household clock, particularly in the provinces, until at least the middle of the eighteenth century.

The clock is fitted with a knife edge verge escapement, Plate I/2 and Figure (a). The verge escapement, so tolerant of uneven surfaces, had been superseded by the anchor, Figure (b), as early as 1670 in longcases but would continue popular in bracket clocks until early in the nineteenth century. The backplate of this clock has tulip engraving typical of the period. The clock has two trains, striking and going, each of

10 R.A. Lee in *The Knibb Family, Clockmakers,* notes in a section about Knibb table clock cases: 'Clocks in ebony veneered cases were by far the most popular. The effect of mercurially gilt mounts on an ebony background is certainly the most dignified combination and this predominant fashion continued well into the 18th Century. It is not generally realised that the use of ebony was an extravagant choice in the 17th Century, as it was an imported wood, and to use walnut or other home-grown woods was far less costly.'

11 *The Iden Clock Collection,* P.G. Dawson.

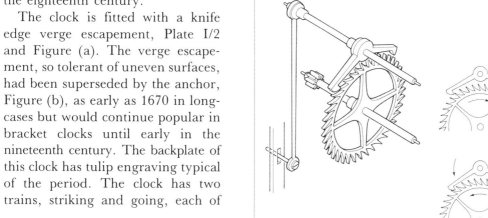

Figure (b) *Anchor escapement.*

eight day duration. Fusées, Figure (c), are employed in each train to maintain an even supply of power as the springs run down, but the most significant difference between this clock and those of the first generation is that by pulling a cord the clock can be made to repeat the hours on the hour bell and the quarters on a smaller bell.

Repeating work is a particularly important feature of English bracket clocks. The most lucid introduction to the subject encountered by the writer was written by C.R.P. Allix as a preface to *Hobson's Choice,* by the late Charles Hobson. It is repeated here by kind permission of C.R.P. Allix and Laurence Harvey.

Figure (c)
Fusée and spring barrel.

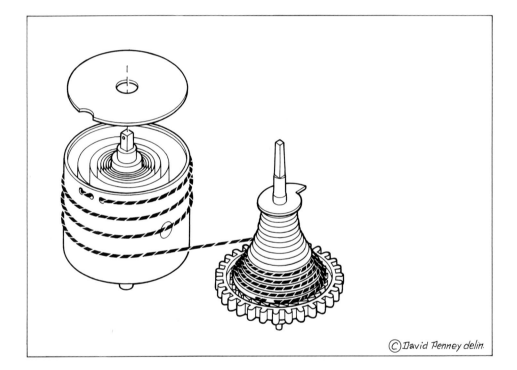

ENGLISH SILENT PULL AND PULL QUARTER REPEATING WORK
by C.R.P. Allix

English spring-clocks, as made from the beginning of the last quarter of the 17th century until late in the 18th, were very often furnished with repeating. This most ingenious and useful adjunct was provided mainly for use after dark and especially when the last light had been extinguished. By simply pulling a cord, the time shown by a clock could be sounded on bells to the nearest quarter of an hour. In an age of primitive lighting (not to mention the inordinate difficulty of igniting in the dark a sulphur "match" from a tinder-box in order to light a candle) the invention must have seemed to many who did not sleep well like the answer to a prayer. The only previous timetellers designed for the hours of darkness had been night clocks. Their rarity today suggests that few were made which did not end in flames.

Most English spring-clocks were designed to be portable. They were highly prized and were carried from room to room very much more than is now generally realised.

Their tolerant verge escapements, light pendulum bobs and sensible top carrying handles well fitted them for duty by day and night. They could be put down on any level-ish surface and there would continue to go reasonably well even when much out of beat. Carried with care they would not stop while being moved. The invention of repeating naturally revolutionised the usefulness of such clocks. Even greater importance came to be attached to them. When later, presumably in the 19th century, the same clocks had their repeating torn out and discarded, it was a symptom of ignorance and incompetence as well as a sign of the times.

Many 17th century spring-clocks were timepieces. That is to say they had only a watch-part (going train) and did not strike. Others had both a watch-part and a clock-part (hour striking train and appurtenances) and struck the hours in passing. Yet others again struck in passing the hour at the hour and the quarter at the quarter. These were known as quarter clocks or three part clocks. At first, and before the invention of repeating, all English striking trains were controlled by count-wheels (locking plates). These advanced inexorably and therefore semed to offer no possibility for repetition. The picture only changed in the reign of Charles II when in about 1676 Barlow and Quare produced clock repeating controlled by snails. From then onwards many spring-driven timepieces, hour striking clocks and quarter clocks, using the new invention, could at will be made to repeat hours and quarters. In timepieces the feature came to be known as silent pull and in hour striking clocks pull quarter. The required results were achieved in a number of different ways. Meanwhile, before the turn of the century, racks and snails superseded locking plates as controllers of striking work in most English clocks, whether spring or weight driven, bracket or longcase. Occasionally a transitional bracket clock will be found having hour striking on a locking plate; yet it will have a completely independent silent pull.

Silent pull and pull quarter clocks were soon followed by quarter and half-quarter repeating watches. These gradually superseded the bracket clock in the bedroom.

The following are the main forms of repeating work as found in English spring-clocks.

(1) Timepieces with Silent Pull

Here, when the cord is fully pulled and then released the last hour is first struck on the hour bell. It is followed by the last quarter sounded on a separate quarter bell or bells. The term ''pull repeating'' often used in connection with silent pull is something of a misnomer since the clock does not strike of its own accord. The silent pull is very ingenious. A subsidiary spring, cocked or wound by the pull only when required, drives a train of wheels known as the runners thereby sounding to the nearest quarter of an hour the time shown by the hands. The earliest clocks, except for those made by Tompion, have no ''all-or-nothing'' piece. As a result a ''short'' pull, depending upon its length, will cause incorrect hours to be struck, or even quarters with no hours. The spring which drives a repeating train is sometimes a straight blade spring, cocked by the pull and then held by clickwork, and sometimes a miniature mainspring housed in a fixed-barrel and wound by pulling off a line wrapped round a deep pulley squared on to the barrel arbor. In general, blade springs are found mostly in striking clocks and coiled springs in timepieces. The reason is that silent pulls have more work to do than pull quarters. After about 1710, blade springs were used less and less as more quarter bells became fashionable. Tompion is only once known to have used a coiled spring in his repeating work (Symonds *Tompion,* fig. 205). In his ''Mostyn'' clock going for a year Tompion employed two ''V''-shaped springs to drive his pull quarter. This form had long been used by locksmiths and gunmakers.

Many of the first table or bracket clocks with silent pull were beautifully small and light. This, coupled with the fact that they did not strike in passing, made them ideal for use upstairs. For this reason many people must have preferred them to hour striking clocks with pull quarter which were not only far heavier but also required setting to ''not strike'' at night if they were to hold their peace.

(2) **Hour Striking Clocks with Pull Quarter**

Here, when the cord is fully pulled and then released, the last quarter is sounded first on one or more quarter bells. Next the last hour is struck on the hour bell. In these clocks the rack striking work for the hours is already present. It requires only initially to be ''warned'' and subsequently released after the pulled-quarters, provided by a separate spring and wound only for the occasion, have been sounded. The striking train is designed not only to sound the hours in passing for a full eight days but also to allow for frequent repetition of the hours. There is then no danger of the striking part running down before the going part. In the ''Mostyn'' clock not only will the going trains run for 384 days but the striking train has the capacity to cover 420 days provided that the repeating work is not used. This allows 20.7 extra blows per day over a 365 day year. The clock was ordered by William III and is undoubtedly Tompion's masterpiece. It is mechanically-speaking the finest clock extant. Its making required incalculably greater precision of design and execution than any year-going weight driven clock. It certainly would not be conceived and made today.

(3) **Quarter Striking Clocks with Pull Repeating**

Here, when the cord is fully pulled and then released, the last quarter is sounded followed by the last hour. In this sort of clock both hour and quarter trains are already present (sometimes one train sounds both hours and quarters, then it is termed three parts in two). All that is necessary in an ordinary quarter clock in order to provide repeating is a means of sequential ''warning'' and release together with adequate resources to sustain the extra blows. The release in this case requires only a very short ''pull'' as no winding-up is involved.

Bracket clocks made in the 1690s tended to be more sophisticated than John Knibb's clock. The ebony clock by Simon de Charmes shown in Plate I/3 has small side apertures above the usual tall apertures in each side of the case. It is thought that these apertures usually contained silk-backed wooden or metal frets which allowed the sound of the bells to be heard. Wooden frets were almost invariably broken and were often replaced by glass but it is likely that some clocks started life with glass-filled apertures, which allowed the movement to be seen. Design changes to the dial include a mock pendulum aperture and a minute band set well within the chapter ring. The minute numbers are now set outside the minute band but the double figure numbers are still divided by an engraved line. In addition to the quarter and half hour markers shown on the inner edge of the chapter ring there are half quarter hour markers shown outside the band. The arrowhead design of the half hour and half quarter hour markers is early and is seldom seen on clocks made after about 1700. The wheatear engraving on the edge of the dial plate is another feature often found on the dials of high quality clocks. The clock strikes the hours and has pull-quarter repeating on three bells. Unusually, perhaps a legacy of Simon de Charmes' French Huguenot origin, the clock also strikes one blow on the hour bell at the half hour.

By the end of the century bracket clock dials were becoming taller. Charles Gretton's elegant repeating clock, Plate I/4, is veneered with prince's wood. It retains its original metal side frets. A number of early clocks exist with prince's wood cases. Prince's wood should not be confused with kingwood which was used later in the eighteenth century. Early clocks are also seen with cases veneered with tortoiseshell, often contrasted with silver mounts, olivewood, walnut and, very rarely, marquetry. It will be noted that the minute figures of Charles Gretton's clock are larger and no longer divided by engraved lines.

Circa 1695, Thomas Tompion began to fill the upper part of his taller dial plates with two subsidiary dials which were used for rise and fall regulation and strike/silent, Plate I/5. This clock retains its original metal frets in the upper side windows but has lost the larger frets from its lower windows. The backplate, Plate I/6, is of particular interest. It shows Tompion's well-known layout, by which the pull-repeat could be operated from either side. The rise and fall work can also be seen clearly. Note the pivoted verge

PLATE I/3 *Simon de Charmes. Clocks of the 1690s were more sophisticated. Mock pendulum aperture, minute band set in from chapter ring edge. Half-quarter hour markers. Ebony case has additional top side apertures.*

PLATE I/4 *Charles Gretton. Dials and cases were often made taller towards the end of the century. Often more brass mounts, minute numerals larger. This example is veneered with prince's wood.*

escapement, this was also a feature of the de Charmes clock shown earlier. The pivoted, as opposed to the knife edge, verge is theoretically inefficient but in practice works well in a well-made clock. It was used by Tompion and several other makers before the end of the seventeenth century.[12] It will also be noted that the engraving style has changed. There are, of course, considerable variations in engraving but the open tulip style shown on John Knibb's clock and the leafy scroll style shown on Tompion's clock are both typical of their periods. The last two clocks shown have taller dials but one of the features of bracket clocks is that there is a considerable overlapping of styles. The square dial, for instance, will continue to appear until *circa* 1725, though a later example will be betrayed by a later spandrel pattern such as the example shown in Plate I/7. John Bridger's clock, which repeats on six bells, was made *circa* 1710. The large crown with crossed maces spandrel (Cescinsky and Webster pattern 10), followed the twin cherub and crown pattern (C. & W. No. 8) which appeared at the beginning of the eighteenth century but is seldom, if ever, seen on bracket clocks. Conversely pattern 10, which first appeared *circa* 1710, is fairly frequently found on bracket clocks but is rarely found on longcase dials. Another feature which shows the later date of Bridger's clock is the style of the half hour markers, larger and more flamboyant than the earlier arrowhead designs.

Two more features which appeared during the early years of the eighteenth century are the inverted bell-top case and the arch dial.

The timepiece repeating ebonised bracket clock shown in Plate I/8 is by Christopher Gould. The inverted bell-top and later half hour markers allow us to date it circa 1710 rather than 1700, though it retains the familiar square dial and cherub spandrels of the earlier period. The inverted bell-top was a forerunner of the bell-top. It first appears in the 1700-10 period but although the bell-top is a familiar feature of bracket clocks made in the second half of the eighteenth century, the clock shown in Plate I/9, if in unaltered condition, suggests that the design originated many years earlier.

Claudius Du Chesne's clock, Plate I/9, shows an early form of bell-top. The square dial has four subsidiaries, rise and fall regulation, strike/silent, day of the month and months of the year and day of the week. The clock is quarter chiming, pull-repeating and month going. It has bolt and shutter maintaining power. Maintaining power, which ensured that power continued to be supplied to the going train while the clock was being wound, is a great rarity in bracket clocks. Claudius Du Chesne, an immigrant Parisian Huguenot maker of exceptional ability, worked in London from 1693 until 1730. This is a large clock, 30 inches high, with a dial width of 9¾ inches. It is also exceptionally heavy; hence the lifting handles attached to the sides. This is not a clock that would have been moved often. It would have been sensible, particularly in view of the maintaining power, to have fitted it with the more accurate anchor escapement but, as is normally the case with bracket clocks of the period, it has verge escapement. The case is of ebonised pearwood. The clock can be dated *circa* 1705.

The low arch tortoiseshell bracket clock by William Ferrar of Pontefract,

12 It is sometimes suggested that the pivoted verge was not used until well into the eighteenth century. A. Woodburn, and no doubt many others including the writer, have seen a number of authentic seventeenth century examples.

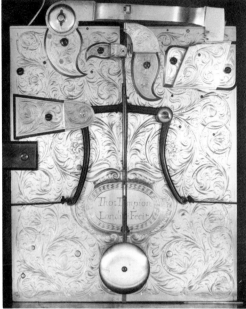

PLATE I/5 *Thomas Tompion number 244. Tompion used the taller dial for strike/not strike and rise and fall subsidiary dials.* Circa *1697.*

PLATE I/6 *Leafy scroll-engraved backplate of Tompion number 244. Note pivoted verge escapement used by Tompion and others pre-1700. Much use of cocks. Levers of pull-repeat system operated from either side.*

PLATE I/7 *Bridger. Styles in bracket clocks often overlap. Diamond half quarter hour markers, later half hour markers, handle style and spandrels betray the fact this clock dates* circa *1710, yet early case style and square dial are retained.*

PLATE I/8 *Christopher Gould. Square dial and early cherubs still retained but case top now of inverted bell shape. Timepiece with pull-repeat. Typical early key.* Circa *1710.*

PLATE I/9 *Claudius Du Chesne. Large, month-going, quarter chiming, repeating clock. Bolt and shutter maintaining power. If the top of the case is unaltered and original it is an extremely early example of a bell-top case.* Circa *1705.*

Plate I/10, was made in 1707. The inscriptions at the top and bottom of the dial have been translated[13] as follows: 'A wise man always has his fortune in council. Buckley Wilsford holds me under the law.' At the bottom of the dial: 'William Ferrar created this, 28th June, 1707.'

This intriguing clock is a particularly early example of provincial work. The transitional low arch would not have been out of place in London at that time but the engraved spandrel corners, a feature we shall see again in the north, were already an old fashioned feature in London by 1680. The engraving style is reminiscent of the 1680-90 period. The theme is repeated on the backplate, Plate I/11. The clock has countwheel striking, though it should be remembered that the countwheel was still being used by London makers during this period on bracket clocks that were not fitted with repeating work. The countwheel strike was used less and less often on London eight day longcases after the beginning of the eighteenth century, though its use persisted in the provinces for much longer. Indeed in the north-west it could still be found in eight day clocks made towards the end of the eighteenth century. Countwheel striking was the norm in thirty hour clocks.

13 Brian Loomes. Article in *Clocks* magazine, June 1984.

The case of William Ferrar's clock is of red tortoiseshell. It is of the true break-arch pattern which did not start to appear in London (and then rarely) until some fifteen years later. The handle is of a later period and must be a replacement. Nonetheless there is no reason to doubt the originality of the case. This is the work of a provincial cabinetmaker working in isolation. By chance he anticipated a case design that would become very popular several decades later. William Ferrar of Pontefract is a well-documented maker, though it is not known to whom he was apprenticed. Buckley Wilsford, a local gentleman, was the clock's first owner.

The penultimate clock in this series of pre-Georgian clocks was probably made at much the same time as William Ferrar's clock. Joseph Windmills was a prolific and successful maker but this example, Plate I/12, which is one of

PLATE I/10 *William Ferrar, Pontefract. An early provincial clock dated 1707. Engraved spandrel corners. Transitional low arch. The tortoiseshell case is a very early example of the break-arch design.*

PLATE I/11 *The backplate of William Ferrar's clock.*

PLATE I/12 *Joseph Windmills. A transitional clock. Arched side apertures and low arch dial, yet retains the domed top.* Circa *1710.*

PLATE I/13 *(left) John Bushman. An ebonised chiming alarum clock with transitional low arch in a very early bell-top case. Height 11½ ins. (29.2cm).* Circa *1710.*

several similar clocks he made during this period, is stylistically a variation of a typical rectangular dialled clock from the end of the seventeenth century. The only differences in the case are the provision of arched side windows and an arched top to the front door. The only difference in the dial is that a low arch replaces the rectangular design such as that shown in Plate I/4.

This is clearly a transitional clock but one of the features of bracket clocks is that earlier case details often reappear many years later. Nonetheless, the dial details and the engraving of the backplate will usually be right up to date; the experienced observer will be able to ascribe the clock to its correct period.

CHAPTER TWO

The Georgian Period
1714-1760

PLATE II/1 *John Knibb, Oxford. Typical clock of the 1715 period. Arch fitted with alarum work. Rectangular side apertures to the case.*

If there is one feature, above all others, which proclaims that a bracket clock belongs to the pre-eighteen hundred Georgian period it is the arch dial. True, there are numerous exceptions, but generally speaking eighteenth century Georgian bracket clocks have arch dials.

The just pre-Georgian transitional low arch example by Windmills, Plate I/12 at the end of the last chapter, showed that Windmills had accepted the arch as a stylistic advance but had failed to appreciate that a taller arch looked better and that the arch could be useful as well as decorative. We can imagine him telling his engraver that he had made a clock with the new-fangled arch dial and that he, the engraver, had better make a good job of filling the space with engraving and the name. In fact the transitional low arch dial did not lend itself easily to any other treatment. What is rather surprising is that several makers produced clocks with the transitional low arch several years after Tompion and Banger, with whose work they must have been perfectly familiar, had already produced two grande sonnerie clocks, numbers 422 and 436,[1] with fully developed arches. These two clocks are thought to have been made as early as 1706.[2] Tompion had already used a fully developed arch for calendar work in the dial of a longcase made for William III *circa* 1695. Tompion and Banger used the arch to show the calendar work and flanked the calendar work with spandrels on both the grande sonnerie bracket clocks.

1 *Thomas Tompion. His Life and Work,* R.W. Symonds.
2 Dating chart of Tompion clocks. *Clocks and Their Value,* Donald de Carle.

31

The first true Georgian bracket clock to be examined, Plate II/1, has a fully developed arch and is signed John Knibb, Oxon. It can be dated *circa* 1715. The Knibb family were noted for the functional and graceful appearance of their clocks but this late example, though a handsome piece, could just as easily have been made by any one of several good makers of the period. In fact it was made by Samuel Aldworth, whose name appears under the tablet bearing John Knibb's name on the dial. Aldworth was John Knibb's first apprentice, and worked for him for a further fifteen years. Eventually he went to London. He was closely associated with both Joseph and John Knibb and is thought to have married John's daughter Elizabeth.[3] Much of his work is indistinguishable from that of the Knibbs and he must have made many of their clocks. This example was no doubt ordered from Aldworth and sold by John during the years of his semi-retirement. John Knibb died in 1722 on July 19th, as his friend Hearne the antiquary recorded in his diary.[4]

The height of this clock is 18½ inches and the dial width 7 inches. The arch features an alarum setting dial but the outer little chapter ring with Roman numerals is entirely decorative. This is a striking clock and the hours and quarters can be pull-repeated. The cherubs in the arch are a pleasing feature that is found on a number of bracket clock dials made between about 1715 and 1730. It is also found, rarely, on longcase clocks. Wheatear engraving is seen less often as time went on and is fairly rare after about 1730. Half quarter hours are still shown. The lozenge shaped half hour markers used in the arch are often associated with George Graham, though Tompion used them earlier on a number of bracket clocks as well as the longcase he made for the Pump Room in Bath in 1709.[5] 'Woman's head' and 'Old man's head' spandrels were both used at the beginning of the eighteenth century before the start of the Georgian period. Both continued in use until *circa* 1740 or later. The hands of this clock are probably original. It will be seen that the hour hand is slimmer than its seventeenth century forbears. The date on most bracket clocks of this period is shown in a square above six o'clock. On this clock it is shown below twelve o'clock, a position often preferred by the Knibbs.

The inverted bell-top ebonised case still retains flat topped side apertures with small side frets above. The handle, of a simpler pattern than that used on the earlier John Knibb shown, is of a style that remained popular, with small variations, for at least a further twenty years.

John Knibb's clock is described in some detail because it is typical of its style and period. John Bushman's clock, Plate II/2, is similar in style but the side apertures of the case are arched, instantly giving the clock a more graceful appearance. The arch is once more used to house an alarum setting dial, the centre of which is blued. The cherubs in the arch are of an even more unusual pattern than those shown on the John Knibb clock. The spandrels are of the twin maces and crown pattern. The hands are probably original.

Plate II/3 shows the movement of Bushman's clock. The hour bell is also used for the three alarum hammers which are driven by a pin wheel. The alarum is wound by pulling the cord wrapped round the grooved pulley visible bottom left in the photograph. The movement pillars and wheel collets are

3 *The Knibb Family of Clockmakers*, R.A.Lee.
4 *Clockmaking in Oxfordshire*, C.F.C. Beeson.
5 *Thomas Tompion. His Life and Work*, R.W. Symonds.

PLATE II/2 *John Bushman. Arched side apertures give the case a more graceful appearance. Arch fitted with alarum work.* Circa *1715.*

PLATE II/3 *(below) Movement of Bushman's clock showing unusual pin wheel driven alarum work and drive to alarum setting disc in the arch.*

PLATE II/4 *(below left) Backplate of Bushman's clock shows engraving typical of the period.*

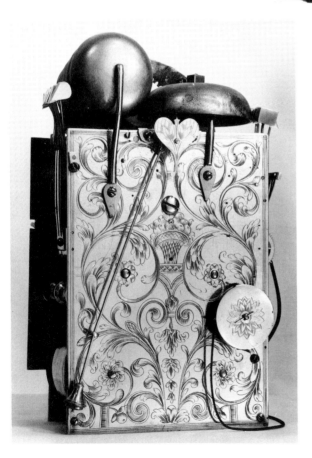

PLATE II/5 *(above) Daniel Quare. Magnificent clock. Arch used for calendar work. Double basket top and original brass mounts. Ex. Iden Collection.* Circa *1715.*

PLATE II/6 *(left) John Naylor. Timepiece pull-quarter repeating on three bells. Ebonised case. Unusual day of week feature.* Circa *1720.*

typical of the early Georgian period. Plate II/4 shows the backplate with its fine leafy scroll engraving, strap work and basket of plenty. The clock pull-repeats on six bells and is secured in its ebonised case by three latches, two of which are visible in Plate II/3. At this time latches such as these were commonly used to secure clocks in their cases. They were usually employed in conjunction with one or more screws that passed through the bottom of the case into the lower movement pillars. Small clocks such as this example, which stands 14¾ inches tall, often dispensed with the screws.

John Bushman was highly regarded. A contemporary description ran as follows.[6]

> 'We reached London at dinner time, that is after 2 o'clock, and in the afternoon we drove to the celebrated clock maker's Buschmann. He is a German and had been established first in The Hague and then for many years in England; he makes as good clocks as Quare's or even Tompion's which are much more expensive...'

6 *Thomas Tompion. His Life and Work,*
R.W. Symonds.

PLATE II/7 *View of the well-made movement of a timepiece pull-repeating clock by a noted early provincial maker; Abraham Weston of Lewes. Circa 1720 (The lacquered case is shown in Plates III/1 and VII/15.)*

PLATE II/8 *Another view of Abraham Weston's movement. Note the ringed early movement pillars and heavy collets.*

John Bushman is believed to have worked until 1725.

Daniel Quare was the maker of the fine double basket top clock shown in Plate II/5. It retains its original brass mounts, feet and side frets. The arch here is used to indicate the date. The clock pull-repeats on six bells and has typical hands. It is numbered 41. Percy Dawson noted[7] that the brass mounts were originally gilded, though these are now polished brass. He noted too that the

7 *The Iden Clock Collection*, P.G. Dawson.

side apertures are of the break-arch pattern and that the arch dial is fully developed. Iden dated this clock *circa* 1710 but Percy Dawson believed it was made no earlier than 1715 and possibly later. Daniel Quare went into partnership with Horseman in 1718; evidently the clock was made before then.

The lacquered case of an early provincial clock by Abraham Weston of Lewes is shown in Plates III/1 and VII/13. The general design of the case is very similar to the John Knibb clock, Plate II/1. It will be seen that the spandrels, including those in the arch, are virtually identical, possibly the dial furniture for both clocks came from the same specialist supplier in London. The hour hands are similar too and are typical of the early Georgian period. This is a particularly interesting provincial clock that had until recently never travelled further than six miles from where it was made. It has survived in virtually untouched condition. Plates II/7, II/8 and II/9 show views of the dial, movement and backplate. The clock is a timepiece, pull-repeating the hours on one bell and the quarters on a second bell. The movement is finished to a high standard. The engraving is excellent. The false pendulum bob in the arch is not a country touch. It occurs on London clocks with arch dials

PLATE II/9 *The backplate of Abraham Weston's clock showing the engraving and original backcock apron.*

too. An example can be seen in Colour Plate 14.

Abraham Weston's shop stood at what is now 77 High Street in Lewes. He was born in Mayfield in 1676 and was working before the end of the seventeenth century. His wife's sister and his daughter both married clockmakers.[8] His son, grandson and many Gilmore and Body relations[9] were also clockmakers. Abraham Weston was also a gunmaker. E.J. Tyler, the authority on Sussex clocks, believes that this clock, which must have been made in the 1715-20 period, is the oldest surviving Sussex bracket clock. Abraham Weston died in 1746. Unfortunately it is not known to whom he was apprenticed.

The fine walnut bracket clock, Colour Plate 2 and Plate II/10, was made by John Sanderson of Wigton in Cumberland *circa* 1715. The clock is evidently very well made and finished. It strikes the hours and pull-repeats the hours and quarters. The backcock appears to be of a later style and may be a replacement, as, probably, are one or more of the bells. Bells throughout the Georgian period were left either rough-cast or polished but would all originally

8 *The Early Clockmakers of Great Britain*, B. Loomes.
9 *The Clockmakers of Sussex*, E.J. Tyler.

PLATE II/10 *(right) Movement and backplate of Sanderson's clock. Excellent work but repeat bells and backcock apron are probably replacements.*

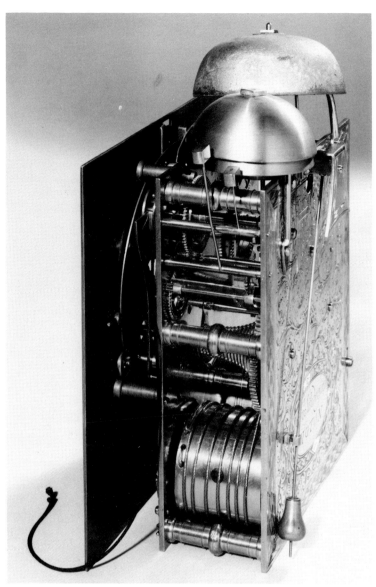

PLATE II/11 *(left) Claudius Du Chesne. Double basket top clock. Lunar dial and lunar day, day of the month, day of the week, strike/silent, rise and fall regulation. Finely engraved dial. Fine brass mounts.* Circa *1715.*

have been of the same type on one particular clock.

The square dial of this clock has a fine wheatear engraved border surround and engraved spandrel corners. Longcase clocks with no spandrels, engraved spandrels or spandrel corners or dial centres containing apposite sayings were quite common in the north. Usually they were the work of Quaker makers. A typically depressing example, found on another clock by John Sanderson,[10] who was probably a Quaker, runs as follows:

> 'Behold this hand,
> Observe ye motions trip
> Man's pretious hours
> Away like these do slip.'

10 *The Clockmakers of Cumberland,* J.B. Penfold.

37

PLATE II/12 *Joseph Kirk, Harstoft. The dial of an early provincial pull-repeating timepiece made between 1710 and 1720. Kirk later went to Nottingham.*

PLATE II/13 *Backplate of Kirk's clock. The chapter ring and backplate were almost certainly engraved in London (Verge backcock apron removed).*

PLATE II/14 *Left side view of movement and under dial work of Kirk's clock. Square screws (seen on frontplate) are a typically provincial feature.*

PLATE II/15 *Right side view of movement of Kirk's clock. Unusual form of repeat work.*

PLATE II/16 *Simple walnut case, probably made locally, of Kirk's clock.*

16

12

13

14   15

    The walnut veneered case of John Sanderson's clock has faded over the years to a particularly beautiful tone. The door fret and the frets in the side apertures of the clock appear to be original.

    Another clock which lacks spandrels is shown in Plate II/11. In this instance the spandrel corners and arch have been used for subsidiary dials showing the month and the number of days it contains; the phases of the moon and the lunar day; the day of the week; strike/silent and rise and fall regulation. The day of the month is shown above twelve o'clock. The maker is Claudius Du Chesne. This example must have been made for a French or French speaking client; all the functions on the subsidiary dials are engraved in French. The lunar phase is a rarity on bracket clocks. The method used here, with the moon shown through a small aperture, also appears in the arch of longcase clocks of the early Georgian period. Later, from about 1725, the lunar feature fills most of the arch. An example is shown in a clock by Clarke and Dunster, Plate II/25. Claudius Du Chesne's clock was probably made at about the same time as the Daniel Quare clock shown in Plate II/5. The basket top and the finials appear to have been made by the same trade supplier.

Clocks by provincial makers of this period were usually made by men who worked in towns or cities. The small village makers whose output was largely confined to simple thirty hour longcases had little or no demand for such sophisticated and expensive items as bracket clocks. But one maker who was well placed to take an important order was Joseph Kirk of Harstoft. Harstoft, Hardstoft today, is a tiny hamlet on the estate at Hardwick Hall on the Nottinghamshire/Derbyshire borders. The dial of Joseph Kirk's timepiece pull-repeating bracket clock, Plate II/12, suggests a date somewhere between 1700 and 1715. But the engraving of the backplate shows the fully developed form of strapwork which emerged *circa* 1710. Obviously a clock must be dated by its latest feature; this clock was almost certainly made between 1710 and 1720.

Communications in those days were good enough for Kirk to have arranged for the engraving of the chapter ring, and by logical inference the backplate also, to have been carried out in London. The chapter ring, as mentioned in Chapter I, has the name 'Bockett' inscribed on the obverse side. Richard Bockett, the name was originally French, Bouquet, was a member of a well-known London clockmaking family, one of whom was a founder member of the Clockmakers' Company. Bockett had at least one other provincial trade customer, the famous Gabriel Smith of Barthomley in Cheshire. Once again Bockett inscribed his name on the back of a chapter ring.[11] Richard Bockett was working *circa* 1712.[12] The result of his collaboration with Kirk is a clock that could have been made in London if only the dial and backplate, Plates II/12 and II/13 are viewed. But the movement, Plates II/14 and II/15, with its unusual arrangement of the pull-repeat work and the square headed screws which are almost always the hallmark of the small country maker, is obviously Joseph Kirk's own work. Kirk's father had been apprenticed in London in 1668 and was freed in 1677. No doubt this interesting movement was the son's interpretation of an explanation of London pull-repeating work given to him years earlier by his father. The clock appears to be in entirely original condition save for the loss of the backcock apron and the replacement of the verge pallets. The pallets were originally of gut, which made them almost silent in operation. This is a feature which was found in a number of clocks intended for bedroom use. The case of Joseph Kirk's clock, Plate II/16, is a slightly country-looking version of the simple London dome top of some years earlier. It is veneered in walnut and was probably made locally.

Joseph Kirk eventually moved to Nottingham where he died *circa* 1735. There is still a lacquer longcase by him in Hardwick Hall, where no doubt it will remain as it now has a central heating pipe passing through its case. Other longcases by Kirk are illustrated in *English Domestic Clocks* (Cescinsky and Webster) and *The Longcase Clock* (Tom Robinson). The Robinson clock, an early thirty hour example, has a highly individual striking mechanism.

Occasionally a bracket clock is seen which is more exuberant in design. The quarter chiming and musical example shown in Colour Plate 3 is by Simon de

11 Noted by Brian Loomes.
12 *Old Clocks and Watches and Their Makers*, F.J. Britten.

PLATE II/17 *Edward Crouch. Low arch dial and pillared case of a large clock. Spandrels typical of the period. Circa 1715.*

PLATE II/18. *Backplate of Edward Crouch's clock. Rotating discs on back of dial are a normal method of locking the movement into the case during the early Georgian period. The complicated series of levers to lock pendulum are operated from front of clock as is rise and fall regulation.*

Charmes. It would be tempting to suggest that it was made for a fellow Huguenot refugee, but this is unlikely. Some of the Huguenot refugee craftsmen deservedly became extremely prosperous. Indeed Simon de Charmes himself built Grove Hall in Hammersmith. But this exquisite clock, with its exceptional silver mounts, tortoiseshell case and extremely complex movement, must have been beyond the means of even the most prosperous tradesman. It is sobering to reflect that it was made during an age when electric light and power were not available.

The backplate of the clock shown in Plates II/17 and II/18 illustrates the fact that there is nothing new in gadgetry. Edward Crouch's large clock stands 27¼ inches high. It can be seen that there is a complicated system for locking the pendulum should it be necessary to move the clock. The subsidiary dials are engraved with the words 'Lock the swing/Unlock the swing' and 'Strike/Not strike'. The subsidiary dial in the arch is for rise and fall regulation of the pendulum. The engraving of the backplate of this clock is particularly well-executed and is typical of the early Georgian period. The case, with its

PLATE II/19 *(left) George Graham. Tompion's successor. Typical rectangular dial with twin subsidiaries. Inverted bell-top case.* Circa 1725.

PLATE II/20 *(below) Under dial work of Graham's clock. Complicated but smooth running pull-repeat work. Tompion's system. Typically Tompionesque use of cocks and heavily built but beautifully finished parts.*

PLATE II/21 *(below left) Brass hinges of this pattern secured by nails were usual throughout the eighteenth century.*

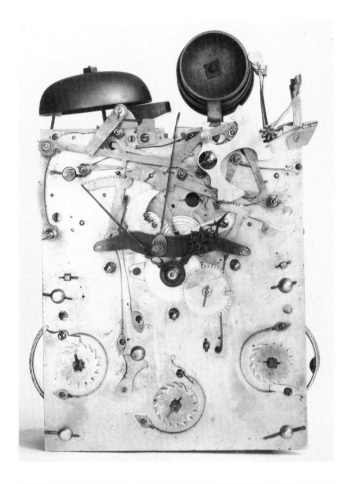

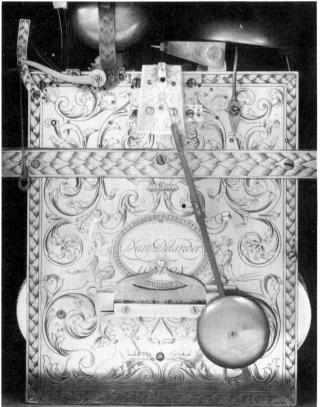

PLATE II/22 *(above left) Under dial work of Daniel Delander's grande sonnerie clock.*

PLATE II/23 *(above) A view of the movement of Daniel Delander's grande sonnerie clock.*

PLATE II/24 *Backplate of Daniel Delander's grande sonnerie clock. Probably later backcock apron. Unusual but effective retaining strap.*

acorn finials, is of particular interest because it has door pillars reminiscent of a longcase clock of the period. This is a design feature that appears from time to time during the Georgian period.

It will be evident that the arch dial was very well established by 1720 but some makers continued to make clocks with square or oblong dials. The best known of them was George Graham, Tompion's successor. Plate II/19 shows a typical production. In Plate II/20 the under dial work of this clock is illustrated. The whole construction is extremely solid with thick plates and much use of cocks. The repeat system is Tompion's, very complex yet beautifully made and delightfully smooth in operation. Plate II/21 shows the clock with the front door open to show the hinges. Hinges, usually brass, were secured with nails throughout the Georgian period. Unfortunately nails tend to work loose and many have since been replaced with screws. A small point of interest is that this clock, like many other good quality examples, has chains rather than gut to transmit the power from the spring barrels to the fusées. A fusée that was originally made to take a chain has grooves that are square cut at the bottom. Fusées for gut have rounder grooves. The spring barrel of a clock made for gut has three holes to allow the securing of the gut. A spring barrel made to take a chain has one hole shaped to take the hook on the end of the chain. Fusée chain making was an arduous task that required exceptionally good eyesight. During the eighteenth century a cottage industry was established in Hampshire to make these chains. The labour force largely comprised women and children in the Workhouse.[13] Their eyes and hands suffered considerably from the work.

Colour Plate 4 and Plates II/22-24 show an important grande sonnerie clock with an oblong dial by Daniel Delander, made probably between 1715 and 1720. Daniel Delander was initially apprenticed to Charles Halsted, one of a well-known family of seventeenth century clockmakers but by 1693 he was with Thomas Tompion. He was Free in 1699 and subsequently worked for Tompion as a journeyman until 1714, when he set up on his own in Devereux Court.

It will be seen that the hands that control the rise and fall and the selection

PLATE II/26 *Daniel Delander. Elaborately brass mounted case, early use of circular apertures above case side apertures. Method of showing minute numerals very old-fashioned indeed by this date. Typical hands and spandrels. Circa 1725.*

PLATE II/28 *John Gordon. A transitional case bridging the gap between the inverted bell and true break-arch case. Circa 1720.*

PLATE II/27 *A view of the original finely engraved brass side frets of Daniel Delander's clock.*

PLATE II/29 *Windmills.*
Mirror glass is used for the
case of this early example of a
true break-arch case. Circa
1720.

of the type of striking are very Tompionesque, while the diamond shaped endings to the quarter hour markers are reminiscent of those employed by Graham. The spandrels, the palm leaf shaped cartouche bearing the maker's name and the central swag suspended by little *putti* are all in silver. The case is of ebony, 17½ inches high. The dial surround is of gilt metal, as possibly was once the sound fret, which appears to be a replacement. The side frets are certainly later replacements but it is not known whether they replace wood or metal frets.

A grande sonnerie clock differs from a quarter striking clock in that at the quarter hours the hour is struck as well as the quarters. Delander's clock allows a choice of grande sonnerie, petite sonnerie (i.e. quarters only at the quarters and the hour at the hour), hours only, or silent. The movement has seven pillars, triple chain fusées, rise and fall mechanism, repeating mechanism and six bells for the quarters. It is solidly made. The engraved fixing strap that runs across the back of the movement is an unusual but effective feature. Delander's work reflects the excellent schooling he must have received at the hands of Tompion and Graham. He is a maker whose work deserves to be better known.

Plate II/25 illustrates a typical 1720s clock by Clarke and Dunster. By this time more brass was being used to ornament the cases. In this instance there are large brass finials and brass around the door and sound apertures. The lunar dial, a rarity on bracket clocks, is now of the type that will remain in use until the end of the period.

A second clock by Daniel Delander is similar, Plate II/26. Unusually, it has retained all its original engraved brass side frets. This is an early example of the use of round sound apertures above the usual side apertures, Plate II/27.

The clock illustrated in Plate II/28 is obviously transitional. It bridges the gap between the inverted bell-top and the true break-arch. Interestingly the dial design with the two subsidiaries placed to each side of the arch is also one that will become popular with better makers later in the century. Indeed, if the super-structure were removed from the ebonised

PLATE II/30 *The backplate of Windmills' mirror glass clock.*

case the clock would look very similar to a clock made forty years later by Vulliamy, for example. The maker, John Gordon, was working 1698-1723; this must have been one of the last clocks he made.

The break-arch case did not really come into its own until well into the second half of the eighteenth century, though it has remained popular until the present day.

The Windmills family were famous clockmakers for more than sixty years. They have now been the subject of much research, from which it is evident that some of them also became extremely rich.[14] The bracket clock shown in Plate II/29 is unusual in that the case is made of mirror glass and has a break-arch top, an early example. Plate II/30 shows the backplate. The basket of plenty is still a popular theme but the engraving shows no signs of strap work, although strapwork will continue to feature until mid-century. Plate II/31 shows an even more elaborate example of the use of mirror glass. The clock, which is musical, is by William Webster of Exchange Alley. The galleried top to the case is a feature which will reappear.

14 *Antiquarian Horology.*

The last years of George I's reign and the early years of the reign of George II were clearly years of experimentation for the men who made the clock cases. The greater use of brass to form a contrast with the ever popular black cases, the use of architectural features such as columns, the employment of intricate brass castings as ornamentation on more important pieces, lacquer cases (dealt with in a separate chapter), a greater diversity of case styles, the demand from the Near East for more elaborate pieces, these are all factors which confirm that the clock was becoming a decorative piece of furniture in addition to being a useful artefact. However, it is surprising that mahogany does not appear to have been used as a case material for either longcase or bracket clocks until about 1750.

Mahogany had been known in Europe since at least 1662. Catherine of Braganza married Charles II in that year and her dowry included a cargo of mahogany.[15] The import duty on mahogany arriving in Britain was lifted in 1721 and its use for furniture was common enough by 1730. Why then no early mahogany clock cases? One explanation is that mahogany was difficult to work. Another, more likely, explanation is that the majority of clock buyers during the pre-1750 period and indeed the majority of clockmakers themselves, were very conservative. There was already a well-established demand for longcases with walnut, lacquered, ebonised or oak cases (though oak appears to have been scarcely, if at all, used for eight day longcase clocks in London) and for bracket clocks with ebony, ebonised, walnut, lacquered, tortoiseshell or kingwood cases. But the top makers who provided the more decorative clocks made from the more unusual materials, an elite group, nearly all of whom worked in London, must have been catering to the same wealthy patrons who would have ordered furniture in the new material, mahogany. Nonetheless early Georgian mahogany bracket clocks are not just rare. They are effectively non-existent.

The question remains largely unanswered but it is abundantly clear, to judge from the large number of authentic surviving examples, that bracket clocks with black cases were by far the most popular choice until mahogany became really popular in the second half of the eighteenth century. Even then, and indeed until the end of the Georgian period, black bracket clock cases were made in considerable numbers. What is generally not realised is that walnut veneer was never extensively used for bracket clock cases during the Georgian period and was used even less for bracket clocks during the immediate pre-Georgian period. This is evidenced by the fact that Tompion's considerable production of bracket clocks includes only one example in walnut. Tompion was the leading and most successful maker during the immediate pre-Georgian period. If there had been a strong pre-Georgian demand for walnut veneered bracket clocks then we may be sure that many more walnut bracket clocks by Tompion would be known today. In fact it is clear, judging again from the many authentic surviving pre-Georgian examples, that ebony or ebonised pearwood was already established as the most popular veneered finish for good quality bracket clocks with tortoiseshell, princes wood and very rarely lacquer as occasional and costly alternatives.

It can be accepted that black makes a particularly effective contrast with the gold and silver of a bracket clock dial but it is rather overwhelming if used for a longcase, hence the preference for longcases in walnut or walnut marquetry during the pre-Georgian period. In fact many more black (usually ebonised

15 *The Story of English Furniture*, B. Price.

COLOUR PLATE 1 *James Tunn. A finely engraved ebony veneered clock. Tunn was a journeyman who worked for Tompion. Circa 1715.*

pearwood) longcases were made both during the pre-Georgian period and during the early pre-mahogany Georgian period than is now realised. Tompion made many such clocks. Unfortunately the popularity of walnut today has led to many black longcases, including several of those by Tompion, being re-veneered with walnut. There can be no doubt that many black bracket clock cases have received the same treatment. If the work was well done and has had time to acquire some age and patina it can be extremely hard to detect.

The apparent non-existence of early mahogany bracket clocks, even allowing for the continuing popularity of black clocks, is made even more puzzling by the fact that walnut, at first sight the obvious rival to mahogany, was itself becoming scarce by the start of the Georgian period. As we have seen, walnut was a popular choice for better longcase clocks and furniture during the immediate pre-Georgian period. But in 1709 a particularly severe winter destroyed most of the walnut trees in Britain and Europe. By the start of the Georgian period much of the existing stock had been used up. The only walnut available was from felled maturing timber that had already been put

COLOUR PLATE 2 *John Sanderson. Wigton, Cumbria. A square dial inverted bell-top walnut veneered case of particular beauty. Engraved spandrels. Noted early provincial maker.* Circa *1715.*

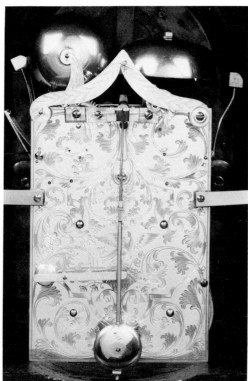

PLATE II/32 *William Scafe. An unusual and effective dial design for a handsome clock. Circa 1730.*

PLATE II/33 *The backplate of William Scafe's clock showing the individual design of the rise and fall mechanism. The retaining straps are almost certainly later additions.*

aside by the more prudent merchants and joiners or new timber from the much depleted stock of trees. The result was that by the start of the Georgian period walnut was reserved for the best longcases and, due perhaps to its now rarer and more expensive status, was used occasionally for good quality bracket clocks.

Given this shortage of walnut it is inexplicable that clock casemakers did not turn with relief to the new wood, mahogany. But one more factor that may help to explain the situation is that the early Georgian period did not see a time of sustained financial growth, and thus an increased demand for luxury goods, such as was seen during the later Georgian period. Elizabeth White, formerly of the Victoria and Albert Museum, in a conversation with the writer, suggested that during the 1730-60 period at least a part of the demand was filled by the first generations of inherited and second-hand clocks that must by then have been appearing on the market. It must also have been the case that the lacquer clocks, then in the ascendancy, satisfied a good part of the demand.

William Scafe's clock, Plate II/32, is notable for the very striking and individual effect created by the unusual design of the dial. Scafe was a Yorkshire-man, which perhaps accounts for the individualism. It should be pointed out, however, that the dial of Tompion's equation clock made for the Pump Room in Bath as early as 1709 creates much the same effect. Scafe was apprenticed to his father in Yorkshire. He subsequently came to London and became Free of the Clock-makers' Company in 1721. He became Master in 1749. His clock dates *circa* 1730. The ebonised case of this clock, with its five

PLATE II/34 *Godfrey Poy. A very fine musical clock with an ebonised case, brass mounts and engraved brass sound frets.* Circa *1740.*

finials, is similar in feeling to the superstructures of the cases of the arch dial walnut longcases that were being produced in London and the provinces during the 1720-35 period.

The backplate of Scafe's clock, Plate II/33, still contains strapwork within the engraving together with the popular basket of plenty. The levers at the top of the movement appear original. They actuate the rise and fall regulation. The case retaining straps are unengraved and are almost certainly later additions.

Highly engraved backplates were evidently much admired. Indeed they are still admired today but some makers, or perhaps their clients, took the view

COLOUR PLATE 3 *Simon de Charmes. A magnificent example of the clockmaker's art. Quarter chiming, musical clock in an exceptional silver-mounted red tortoiseshell case. Circa 1715.*

COLOUR PLATE 4 *Daniel Delander. Grande sonnerie clock. Silver dial mounts. Delander was apprenticed to Thomas Tompion and afterwards worked for him for many years.* Circa *1720.*

COLOUR PLATE 5 *John Ellicott. Handsome walnut clock with unusual fly-back date feature in the arch.* Circa *1730.*

that an engraved backplate was either an unnecessary expense or was seldom seen and contributed nothing either aesthetically or mechanically towards the function of the clock. It is also possible that some eighteenth century clocks with unengraved backplates were made to stand on wall brackets, i.e. the backplate would not be seen. Whatever the reason some eighteenth century clocks, usually of high quality and made by good makers, will sometimes be found with backplates bearing only the maker's name. But by the beginning of the nineteenth century and, increasingly, as time progressed backplates were left plain or carried only a minimum of border engraving. The unengraved backplate of a clock dated 1754 is shown in Plate II/56.

Godfrey Poy's clock, Plate II/34, is an altogether more graceful example of

PLATE II/35 *Isaac Du Hamel. A clock showing a strong French influence both in its design and decoration. The mounts and dial decoration are rococo. The case is of tortoiseshell with brass inlay (Boulle work). Circa 1735.*

PLATE II/36 *Isaac Du Hamel. A case of similar design to Plate II/35 in ebonised pearwood. Circa 1735.*

a large clock than that shown earlier by Edward Crouch in Plate II/16. It is a musical clock which at every hour or at will plays one of the twelve tunes advertised in the arch. There are thirteen bells and twenty-four hammers. The substantial movement has ten pillars and verge escapement. The ebonised case has fine brass embellishments and graceful fluted brass pillars. The brass frets are particularly noteworthy. The clock stands 30½ inches high.

Colour Plate 5 shows another use for the arch of a walnut clock by the famous John Ellicott. The little dial in the centre of the arch indicates the month itself and the number of days it contains. The periphery of the arch shows the days of the month from 1-31. The pointer flies back to the beginning at the start of each new month. This is one of a series of fine clocks made by Ellicott that differ in mechanical detail but are housed in virtually identical walnut veneered cases.

PLATE II/37 *Windmills. A typical inverted bell-top case but the arcaded dial plate shows the French influence of Daniel Marot.* Circa *1715.*

Plates II/35 and II/36 show two similar but by no means identical clocks by Isaac Du Hamel. Each is fitted with a rise and fall mechanism to regulate the pendulum, and a striking movement with pull-quarter repeating on six bells. The clock in Plate II/35 is of tortoiseshell inlaid with brass and fitted with rococo brass mounts. The second clock, Plate II/36, has an ebonised case. The finely engraved brass side frets are visible in the photograph. Both these clocks have full arch dials and illustrate the wide variety of brass mounts that had become available to the clock casemaker by the 1730s. The dial fittings and case mounts of Du Hamel's clocks are rococo. The rococo influence, which originated in France, was popularised by Chippendale the elder in Britain. The rococo influence will become increasingly apparent in the design of case and dial mounts and backplate engraving but the actual bracket clock cases themselves will be little affected.

The cases of these two Du Hamel clocks show considerable French influence. Du Hamel himself was, of course, of French extraction but English

PLATE II/38 *Isaac Du Hamel. A typical brass-mounted ebony case. The maker's name is signed behind the false pendulum bob.* Circa *1735.*

PLATE II/39 *The backplate of the clock shown in Plate II/38.*

makers, including Tompion, of every period occasionally placed their movements in cases of French design or cases showing much French influence. French features also influenced dial plates. The clock in Plate II/37 is a conventionally cased quarter repeating ebonised bracket clock made at the beginning of the Georgian period by a traditional maker, Windmills, yet the arcaded dial plate clearly derives from a Marot design.[16]

Isaac Du Hamel's usual productions were housed in cases that conformed to normal English taste of the period. Plates II/38 and II/39 show the front and back views of a typical good quality clock of the mid-1730s; the only slight departure from the norm is that the sound frets in the front door are slightly larger than usual, perhaps to allow the sound of the alarum to escape.

The 1740s heralded a number of changes to both dials and cases. Daniel Torin and Moses Fontaine's clock has cast brass decorative corners, Plate II/40. These cast corners will continue as an occasional feature until the end

16 See Plates 13 and 17 in *Nouveaux Livre d'Ornements*. 1703, 1713. Daniel Marot. Illustrated page 438 in *The Pictorial Dictionary of British 18th Century Furniture Design* compiled by Elizabeth White.

PLATE II/40 *Daniel Torin and Moses Fontaine. Quarter chiming clock. Cast brass corners in addition to brass mounts and finials. Lunar dial. Circa 1740.*

PLATE II/41 *Stephen Rimbault. Large musical clock. Dutch wavy minute band. Circa 1745.*

PLATE II/42 *Backplate of Rimbault's clock showing the musical work.*

of the period. Containing the upper half of a human figure they are called terms, if they contain a complete draped figure they are called caryatids. Stephen Rimbault introduces a wavy minute band to the chapter ring, Plate II/41, of his musical clock. This was a popular design feature in Holland. Indeed Stephen Rimbault must have made this clock for a Dutch client because although the sector in the arch which indicates the choice of tune is in English the other dial indications are in Dutch. The wavy minute band occurs occasionally on English longcase and bracket clocks from the 1740s until about 1780. The musical work and backplate of Rimbault's clock are shown in Plate II/42.

Stephen Rimbault was a fine maker who specialised in complicated clocks. Many have automata. An example of a quarter chiming clock with automata is shown in Plate II/43. The wavy minute band is repeated. Some of Rimbault's painted backdrops are the work of the youthful Zoffany, who was for some time Rimbault's decorative assistant. Zoffany painted a picture of Rimbault that pleased him so much that he introduced him to Wilson, the portrait painter. Wilson subsequently employed Zoffany at a salary of £40 per annum to fill in draperies. His ability was recognised by David Garrick who channelled his energies towards theatrical portraiture. Soon his name was made.[17]

The case of Rimbault's clock shows a significant change. It is a true bell-top. The bell-top case started to become popular *circa* 1745 but the emergence of the true bell-top as a popular case style had little effect on the popularity of the inverted bell-top which continued to be made until the end of the eighteenth century. The wavy door of this clock shows some French influence, it is an attractive variation. The feet, see also Plates II/41 and II/42, are of a pattern that will become extremely popular. Stephen Rimbault now signs his name on a plaque applied from the back of the dial plate.

Plate II/44 shows a third clock by Stephen Rimbault. It was made *circa* 1750. This clock is quarter chiming and musical. It is an important piece but a significant innovation is that there are neither half hour markers between the Roman hour numerals nor quarter hour markers engraved round the inside edge of the chapter ring. By now people were becoming accustomed to clocks with minute hands. Naturally, the changeover was slower in the country where less sophisticated people than London-made bracket clock buyers continued to purchase thirty hour cottage longcases or wall or lantern clocks made with only an hour hand and thus showing only the hours and quarter hours. Half-quarter hour markers on two handed clocks seem to have been an option on longcase and bracket clocks from towards the end of the seventeenth century until some time in the late 1730s. They can occur until mid-century or later on provincial two-handed longcase clocks.

Plate II/45 shows a clock by a well-known Yorkshire maker, Henry Hindley of York. Hindley favoured full arch dials for his more important longcases and here transfers the design to a bracket clock. The bottom of the dial is used for the strike/silent lever. The mock pendulum bob in the arch is not a usual Hindley feature though there is no reason to doubt its originality. Plate II/46

17 *Old Clocks and Watches and Their Makers*, F.J. Britten.

PLATE II/43 *Quarter chiming clock with automata for which Stephen Rimbault was noted. True bell-top case.* Circa *1750.*

PLATE II/44 *Rimbault.*
Chiming and musical clock.
Quarter and half hour markers
now absent from the chapter
ring. Arch indications show
that the clock was made for a
Frenchman. Circa 1750.

shows a side view of the movement. The six baluster-shaped pillars are
reminiscent of the work of the famous Knibb brothers working at the end of
the seventeenth century. They are a typical Hindley feature. It will be seen that
the fusées are reversed and are fitted with chains, though the three holes in the
spring barrels suggest the clock was either originally fitted with gut or has been
changed from chains to gut and back to chains again.

Yet another innovation of this period was the use of enamel dials for bracket
clocks. An early example, *circa* 1750, by George Graham, Tompion's

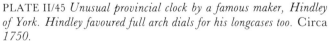

PLATE II/45 *Unusual provincial clock by a famous maker, Hindley of York. Hindley favoured full arch dials for his longcases too. Circa 1750.*

PLATE II/46 *Movement of Hindley clock showing his characteristic baluster pillars.*

successor, is shown in the chapter on lacquer clocks, Plate III/4. Graham died in 1751. Enamel dials were already being used on watches on the Continent in the late seventeenth century and were common on watches in England by 1730. In the early days, difficulty was experienced with the production of larger dials and the costs were high. Thus, although enamel dials were used for bracket clocks in the second half of the eighteenth century and throughout the nineteenth century, they are usually only found in Georgian bracket clocks of good quality.[18]

18 A full explanation of the production methods used in making enamel dials is given in *English Bracket and Mantel Clocks* by Andrew Nicholls.

PLATE II/47 *Side view of John Ellicott's amboyna wood clock showing very fine silver gilt rococo mounts.*

PLATE II/48 *Rear view of John Ellicott's amboyna wood clock.*

PLATE II/49 *The design of this type of case usually used in conjunction with a silvered sheet brass one-piece dial or an enamel dial is attributed to John Ellicott. This is an early example, circa 1755, which retains a matted dial centre and applied chapter ring. Case of ebony veneer with brass mounts.*

COLOUR PLATE 6 *John Ellicott. Very fine amboyna wood clock. Silver chapter ring. Silver-gilt rococo mounts attributed to George Michael Moser. Circa 1750.*

PLATE II/50 *John Berry. A small bracket clock in an exceptionally finely brass-mounted ebony case. Unusual double feet and moulded pediments above the side frets. Circa 1755.*

John Ellicott was a maker of great range and versatility, as is demonstrated by the difference between the amboyna wood example shown in Colour Plate 6 and the ebony clock shown in Plate II/49. Amboyna wood comes from the West Indies. The exceptional rococo silver gilt mounts of this clock are attributed to George Michael Moser.[19] The spandrels and dial decorations are silver gilt and the chapter ring is of solid silver. The movement is of the usual excellent quality one expects from this maker. The design of the case is interesting. It can be described as basically English with strong French overtones, the overall effect is pure rococo.

The clock in Plate II/49 makes a complete contrast, a return to restrained English elegance. It will be seen that the front door of the case is designed to cover the dial, save for that part which actually tells the time. This is an early example by John Ellicott, who is credited with introducing the style. It dates *circa* 1755. The matted dial centre and applied chapter ring are still retained but by about 1760 the design was used with enamel or one-piece all-over silvered sheet brass dials. Silvered sheet brass dials did not achieve their

19 *Old Clocks and Watches and Their Makers*, F.J. Britten. 9th Edition.

PLATE II/51 *David Hatfield, Bosworth. Mahogany veneered cases do not appear to have been much used for bracket clocks before about 1760. This example probably dates from the later 1750s.*

PLATE II/52 *Thomas Hall, Rumsey. An early mahogany veneered case.* Circa *1755.*

greatest popularity until towards the end of the eighteenth century. Their use eventually completely eclipsed the traditional dial with chapter ring and spandrels. An alternative early use of the one-piece dial features an inverted bell-top case with the traditional glazed door exposing the whole of a square dial, but the effect thus produced is altogether less graceful.

The Ellicott design lent itself perfectly to the use of the enamel dial. Most enamel dial examples date from 1760-80. The case design itself was used fairly frequently from the mid-1750s until about 1780.

John Berry's clock, Plate II/50, is small, only 11 inches high. It is an exceptionally fine example of the use of brass mounts combined with ebony casework. The brass frets are also noteworthy. The dial is reminiscent of that by George Cutler dated 1757 shown in Colour Plate 7. This clock probably dates from 1750. The case is a true bell-top, yet the moulded pediment above the arch dial features again above the side frets. The double feet are most unusual. There are a few other clocks with similar casework but those seen by

COLOUR PLATE 7 *George Cutler. A small, 13½ in.*
(34.3cm) high, ebonised inverted bell-top bracket clock signed
and dated 1757.

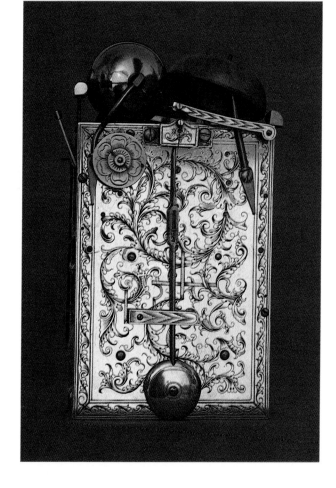

COLOUR PLATE 8 *The backplate of George Cutler's clock*
showing typical engraving, the rise and fall and pull-repeat
pulley mounted on the backplate.

the writer have usually been larger. John Berry is listed as a member of the Clockmakers' Company 1728-54.

The mahogany bracket clock shown in Plate II/51 is a timepiece alarum by David Hatfield of Bosworth in Leicestershire. The common drawer handle is obviously a replacement. David Hatfield was apprenticed in the Clockmakers' Company in London to Francis Corril on the 3rd April, 1732, for seven years.[20] Yet only six years later he is listed working in Bosworth.[21] Francis Corril is listed as a London maker, 1720-32,[22] yet he is listed in Lutterworth, Leicestershire in 1740.[23] It may be assumed that Corril went to Leicestershire some time in the 1730s, taking his apprentice with him. Presumably Hatfield set up on his own in 1738. Possibly both men came from Leicestershire in the first place. David Hatfield's clock was probably made in the 1750s. The dial design owes something to the design of the clock by Scafe shown in Plate II/32.

20 *Register of Apprentices*, Atkins.
21 *Old Clocks and Watches and Their Makers*, F.J. Britten.
22 *Watchmakers and Clockmakers of the World*, G.H. Baillie.
23 *Old Clocks and Watches and Their Makers*, F.J. Britten.

COLOUR PLATE 9 *Colley and Priest. Mahogany bell-top clock. Movement front plate dated 1754.*

Another Scafe clock, a longcase with a similar design feature in the arch, is shown in Tom Robinson's *The Longcase Clock*. Robinson illustrates a second clock with a not dissimilar dial by Seymour of Wantage. Seymour's clock is dated 1752 on the dial plate. As inferred earlier, this dial design almost certainly originally derived from the dial of the equation clock made by Tompion in 1709 for the Pump Room in Bath.

Another mahogany clock that was arguably made in the 1750s is shown in Plate II/52. The rococo spandrels are similar to those on Hatfield's clock. The

PLATE II/53 *Another early mahogany case* circa *1755. The maker, John Smith of York, was apprenticed to Hindley and was working between 1750 and 1764.*

PLATE II/54 *John Ellicott. A brass mounted ebony bracket clock. All-over silvered dial.* Circa *1760.*

maker is Thomas Hall of Rumsey, whom Baillie records with one working date of 1760.

A third early mahogany clock is shown in Plate II/53. The case and dial are similar in design to the Hindley of York clock shown in Plate II/45. This is not surprising as the maker, John Smith of York the elder, is thought to have been apprenticed to Hindley.[24] He was working between 1750 and 1764. The example shown has reversed fusées, alarum work , deadbeat escapement and Dutch striking. The leaf design at the top of the case is also a feature of contemporary mahogany longcase clocks from the north-west. It is interesting to note that the case appears to be the work of Hindley's casemaker. The front door has canted edges, making it invisible from the sides. The writer recalls the same feature on the hood door of the year-going Hindley longcase once owned by him and now in York Museum. It is, of course, a feature of the Hindley bracket clock shown in Plate II/45.

A fourth early mahogany clock is the bell-top example by Colley and Priest

24 R.J. Law, the authority on Joseph Hindley of York.

PLATE II/55 *Front plate of movement of Colley and Priest clock shown in Colour Plate 9. Note Tompion-type repeating mechanism. Colley succeeded Graham, who succeeded Tompion.*

PLATE II/56 *Plain backplate with Tompion-type repeating levers of Colley and Priest clock in Colour Plate 9.*

shown in Colour Plate 9. Interestingly the front plate, Plate II/55, is scratch signed 'J. Bullock 1754'. This, unfortunately, does not show in the photograph, which is included to illustrate the Tompion-type repeating work. Colley and his first partner Barkley, who had been Graham's foreman, were the successors to Graham, who of course had been Tompion's partner and was his successor. Hence the Tompion features in the movement of the clock. Bullock, obviously a chambermaster, i.e. outworker, was almost certainly the James Bullock listed[25] as a clockmaker in Leather Lane. The movement of a burr walnut longcase signed 'Barkley and Colley' is similarly scratch signed 'J. Bullock 1753'. Barkley died in 1753; subsequently Colley went into partnership with Priest. The Tompion and Graham tradition continued because Colley too had worked for Graham, indeed he and Barkley were listed as executors in Graham's Will. Baillie records the partnership of Colley and Priest with a date of 1762, which has led one horologist[26] to suggest that the movement of this bracket clock, made in 1754, was not cased up and signed 'Colley and Priest' until 1762. It seems unlikely that a movement would have been left uncased for eight years. Baillie's 1762 date is possibly a trade directory date. The partnership of Colley and Priest might well have commenced some years earlier. A clock made by Colley during the interregnum is shown Plate VII/4.

25 *Register of Apprentices*, Atkins.
26 Michael Turner, of Sotheby's, in an explanatory note to the description of the Barkley and Colley burr walnut longcase catalogued by Sotheby's in May 1991. Michael Turner noted the scratched dates in the longcase and the bracket clock, illustrated and described herein, and brought them to the writer's attention.

COLOUR PLATE 10 *Joseph Windmills. Very fine cream and dark blue lacquer decorated with delicate flowers and birds.* Circa *1710.*

COLOUR PLATE 11 *George Clarke. Exceptionally large, 36½ in. (92.7cm) high, dark green musical lacquer clock on stepped turntable base.* Circa *1730.*

CHAPTER THREE
Lacquer-cased Bracket Clocks

Bracket clocks with lacquered cases deserve a chapter to themselves, because lacquer played a much more important role in the decoration of eighteenth century clock cases than is generally realised today. Lacquer cases were also a feature of many clocks made for the Turkish market. Several more lacquer bracket clocks are illustrated in **Chapter V. The Export Trade.**

It is believed there are three reasons why lacquer was so popular. First, eighteenth century houses were ill-lit. Lacquer furniture and clocks added brightness and colour to rooms that were often shadowed and gloomy. The second reason was that lacquer conjured up a vision of exotic foreign places. The owners of lacquered furniture, it might be inferred, were travelled, sophisticated people. Third, lacquer filled a gap in the market. Until about 1760, when mahogany started to become widely used for clock cases, there was nothing to fill the gap between the cheaper oak longcase and the, by then, scarce and expensive walnut. In terms of cost, lacquer fell neatly between the two. In addition it was new, exciting, fashionable and different. Lacquer continued to be popular even after the introduction of mahogany, indeed occasional examples are found until early in the nineteenth century, but the heyday for lacquer clocks was between about 1715 and 1770.

A small number of lacquered clock cases were made towards the end of the seventeenth century. It used to be thought that some of these early (late

PLATE III/2 *Robert Coster. Newbury. A good repeating green lacquer clock ripe for restoration. The handle is an incorrect replacement.* Circa *1725.*

PLATE III/3 *John Berry. Exceptional, large lacquer musical clock with automata and cupola top.* Circa *1730.*

seventeenth and early eighteenth century) cases had been sent to the East to be lacquered. The Dutch East India Company offered this service for furniture,[1] but no evidence has come to light to prove that any English clock cases were sent. What is just possible is that some longcase clock doors and plinth panels and possibly some bracket clock cases were made and lacquered in the East and then sent to Europe, but it must be said that the writer has yet to identify any such doors, panels or bracket clock cases.

There is clear evidence that lacquer cabinets and other pieces of lacquered furniture were made in the East to the patterns and order of British entrepreneurs. Indeed the Joiners' Company petitioned Parliament in 1701 to stop the inrush of foreign-made goods which was having an adverse effect on the home manufacturing trade. Their petition read in part as follows:[2]

'The petitioners are very numerous and formerly employed great numbers of the poor...

...there are diverse persons minding only their owne private gain and not having any regard to the good of their own country but desiring rather the ruin and destruction, especially of the handicraft trades (who) take all opportunities of disclosing the said art or mystery be sending models or patterns of the inventions of your petitioners to India[3] and to several other parts from whence great quantities of cabinets, tables, looking glass frames and other Japanned wares after such as your petitioners models or patterns are in India manufactured and dayly imported here, which if not timely prevented will be to the discouragement and total ruin of your petitioners...'[4]

Shortly afterwards, heavy import duties were imposed on foreign-made furniture which presumably slowed down or stopped these imports. In any event, by the start of the Georgian period the European method of imitating the lacquer finish known, perversely, as japanning in Britain, was widely used and understood. We can reasonably assume that all lacquer clock cases of the Georgian period were made and japanned in Britain, but henceforward the writer will refer to these cases as lacquered rather than japanned as lacquer is the word generally used today.

Before examining some examples it is as well to know the difference between the original oriental technique of lacquering and its European imitation. True oriental lacquer, which was first brought to Europe by the Portuguese during the seventeenth century, is rare. The finish was made from the gum exuded by the lac tree (*Rhus Vernicifera*). The resin was coloured black, red, blue, green or yellow and applied to the surface to be lacquered which in turn had had much careful preparation. As many as thirty coats of lacquer might be applied, each being rubbed down and polished before the application of the next coat. The finish was decorated with oriental designs which were often raised and highlighted with gilt. The deep, glossy, hard finish was more durable than the Western imitation.

The European copy of oriental lacquer work was at worst a flat crude

1 *The Longcase Clock*, Tom Robinson.
2 *English Country Grandfather Clocks*, R.C.R. Barder. For a fuller discussion.
3 The word 'India' was used at that time in a broad sense to denote any Eastern country.
4 Guildhall Library London. Manuscript department. M.S. 8046/3.

PLATE III/4 *George Graham. Red lacquer quarter striking bracket clock with an enamel dial, an early example on a bracket clock. Circa 1750.*

business of black and gold paint representing vaguely oriental scenes. At its best it was very fine indeed. The lacquering of a long-case clock would start with the application of a coat of whiting and size, a sort of gesso. When dry and rubbed smooth this was carefully painted with a ground of black, the most popular colour, red, blue, green, cream or even tortoiseshell. A careful balance of oriental designs would be applied to the door, plinth and front of the case using gilding and various subtle colour tones, usually in relief. The sides of the case and hood were lacquered with simpler patterns to form a toning background. Finally, the whole case was carefully varnished and polished.

Lacquer work is susceptible to damp and to being knocked. For these reasons many unrestored cases are in an appalling condition. One frequently applied remedy is to remove all the lacquer from a longcase clock and restain and polish the case which is generally of oak. The experienced observer can usually detect an oak case that was formerly lacquered. Another remedy was to apply several coats of varnish to the lacquer. If this was done many years ago the lacquer work will appear dark and discoloured. Fortunately there are today a number of specialist restorers of lacquer work. A good restorer can work miracles with damaged lacquer and restore an old longcase or bracket clock case entirely sympathetically.

Colour Plate 10 shows a lacquer clock by Joseph Windmills made just before the start of the Georgian period. The case is decorated with delicate flowers and birds in panels of cream on a dark blue ground. This is an excellent example of earlyish lacquer work.

The movement and dial of the black lacquer timepiece repeating clock by Abraham Weston of Lewes was discussed and illustrated in Chapter II. In Plate VII/13 the clock is shown as it was found, i.e. unrestored. Plate III/1 shows the same clock with the lacquer work cleaned and restored. This is a good and particularly original example of provincial lacquer work. The lacquer is applied to a pine carcase, the inside of which has been painted, in this instance with a reddish paint, no doubt to discourage worm. It was normal practice for softwood cases to be so treated.

It has been suggested that lacquer was usually applied to pine cases in the

PLATE III/5 *Claudius Du Chesne. Green lacquer clock case, larger but virtually identical to that shown in Plate III/4.*

provinces and to oak cases, possibly with pine mouldings, in London. There are many exceptions to this rule, though it is true to say that it is unusual to find a pine carcase beneath the lacquer of a London clock.

Plate III/2 shows a green lacquered bracket clock by Robert Coster of Newbury. The handle is of course an incorrect replacement but the clock is otherwise in original condition. It is fitted with pull-repeat on several bells and dates *circa* 1725.

Robert Coster was a notable early Newbury maker,[5] whose tombstone may still be seen at Avington near Newbury. He was apprenticed through the

5 Many of his clocks are described and illustrated in *English Country Grandfather Clocks*, R.C.R. Barder.

Clockmakers' Company in London to Luke Wise of Reading, the son of the
famous John Wise, a seventeeth century London maker. Coster worked in
Newbury from early in the eighteenth century until his death in 1749. Robert
Coster's clock has a pine carcase.[6] The only other Robert Coster bracket clock
known to have survived is also contained in a lacquered case. The clock
illustrated is a good example of a lacquer clock that is ripe for sympathetic
restoration.

George Clarke of Leadenhall Street, London was the maker of the fine dark
green lacquered clock shown in Colour Plate 11. The clock stands 36½ inches.
high and can be revolved on the stepped base. It was made *circa* 1730. The
finials are of facetted crystal. The eight pillar movement strikes the hours on
a bell and plays one of six tunes every three hours, or at will on thirteen bells

6 Georgian bracket clocks, with the
occasional exception of some lacquer
examples, normally have oak carcases.

PLATE III/7 *Ralph Gout.*
Typical later red lacquer clock.
Circa *1775.*

with twenty-five hammers. George Clarke was working from 1725 and was well-known for large important clocks. There was a musical clock by him in the Emperor's Palace in Peking.

The clock by John Berry, Plate III/3, is even more complicated. In addition to being musical it is fitted with automata in the arch. The lacquer work is well drawn and executed. This clock too dates *circa* 1730.

Plate III/4 shows a clock which has a number of points of interest. It is quarter striking and is signed on the backplate. The maker was George Graham, Tompion's partner and successor. The red lacquer case needs cleaning and restoring but appears to have retained most of the original lacquer work. It will be seen that the clock has an enamel dial. George Graham died in 1751 which is about the time that enamel dials were first used on

PLATE III/8 *Frederick Miller. Chelsea. Very late red lacquer clock. A silvered dial is unusual with lacquer. Circa 1820.*

bracket clocks. This clock must have been one of the last to bear his name.

The case is virtually identical to that of a contemporary green lacquer case, Plate III/5, containing an important chiming movement with a lunar dial by Claudius Du Chesne. When this clock was sold by Sotheby's in 1989 it was stated in the catalogue that case and movement had not started life together but there can be little doubt that both cases were made in the same workshop, even though the Du Chesne clock is much larger. The lacquer work is different in design, which may suggest that a finished case was sent by the clockmaker to the artist of his choice who would complete the decoration. The lacquer artist offered a choice of designs and finishes.

It will be seen that, although different designs and standards of finish are found on different clocks, there is no actual progression in the designs used. Clock cases of 1715 are likely to be decorated with much the same styles or designs as those made fifty years later.

Thomas Paye of Norwich made the timepiece red lacquer clock shown in Plate III/6 *circa* 1760. The front door frets are missing, yet the dial mask is lacquered. Lacquer decoration is often found on the dial mask of lacquer clocks. Very often it will be found to be much brighter than the exterior case lacquer because it has been protected by the door. It will thus give a good indication of how the whole case must have looked when new.

Ralph Gout was the maker of the red lacquer bell-top bracket clock shown in Plate III/7. The finials and feet are later additions. Ralph Gout worked in London from 1770 until 1836. He was bankrupt in 1796, when his stock included many watches for the Spanish and Indian markets. This example dates *circa* 1775. Lacquer bracket clocks were made in progressively fewer numbers towards the end of the eighteenth century. Virtually all those that were made still contained clocks with traditional dials, that is to say dials mounted with separate chapter rings and spandrels. Presumably it was thought that the restrained appearance of the all-over silvered dial that was first introduced *circa* 1760 and was popular by the end of the century, was not suited to the flamboyant appearance of lacquer cases. But there are, of course, exceptions to every rule.

The red lacquer clock by Frederick Miller of Chelsea, Plate III/8 is just such an exception. The hatched minute band is a feature found from about 1795 until about 1810. Arabic numerals are a feature rare on brass-dial clocks but common enough on painted-dial longcase clocks made between about 1800 and 1825. The engraving of the silvered brass dial is reminiscent of the spandrel corner painting of some painted dial longcase clocks. Painted dial longcase clocks were very popular by this time, particularly in the north. In the south an expensive longcase clock was still more likely to be fitted with an all-over silvered dial but dial designers did not hesitate to borrow attractive design features from the new painted dials. In *English Country Grandfather Clocks* there was illustrated the silvered dial of a longcase clock made *circa* 1805 by Church Brown of Newtown that is very similar to Frederick Miller's dial. It is likely that books of designs were available which would explain the presence of similar design features on clock dials made in different parts of the country.

We may conclude that Frederick Miller's clock was definitely made in the nineteenth century; the design of the hands, which look original, and are the latest feature, suggest a date *circa* 1820; the case has a mixture of design features but appears to retain its original lacquer.

The point made earlier, that there appears to be no progression in lacquer designs, supports the suggestion that cases were all lacquered by the European method in Britain by the start of the Georgian period. Had cases continued to be lacquered and imported from the East presumably there would have been advances in design and technique. But there is no reason why the best lacquer work carried out in England should not be regarded as an art form on its own; even if it must be admitted, as Arthur Hayden pointed out in *Chats on Old Clocks*:

> ...'It holds the same place in Lacquered work as the Dutch Delft ware does in ceramics. It is a splendid imitation of a technique not grasped by the imitator.'

CHAPTER FOUR

The Georgian Period 1760-1800

The period between 1760 and 1800 was one of considerable activity for the makers of bracket clocks. The first fifteen years or so of this period can be seen to be in one sense a time of gestation and in another, a time of transition between the first period, 1714-60 Georgian clocks and the 1775-1800 period which produced many of the most handsome clocks associated with the Georgian era. That is not to say that beautiful clocks were not produced during the middle years of the eighteenth century; there are many excellent examples; but there are also many exceptions, clocks in which the constituent parts do not blend together to form the harmonious whole we now associate with the best of Georgian clock design.

The three most popular basic designs of the 1760-1800 period proved to be the bell-top, the inverted bell-top and the break-arch but all of them received many different treatments and were subject to so many variations that they are sometimes hard to recognize. Mahogany really came into its own as a case material during the 1760-1800 period but imported red walnut, used sometimes for longcases, was seldom used. From 1775-1800 the case designs already mentioned would be joined by the balloon design, though curiously the latter never became as popular as the excellence of the design would lead us to expect.

The movement was completely taken for granted by 1760 or earlier. The only change to the normal two train clock was that by 1760 far fewer clocks were being made with pull-quarter repeating work on one or more bells. Instead the movement was often made to repeat the last hour on the hour bell only. Alarum work continued to be fitted to a few clocks. Timepieces, i.e. non striking clocks and timepieces with alarum work, continued to be made but far fewer timepieces with pull-quarter repeating work are seen. Quarter striking and musical clocks were also made. Inevitably there were some makers who experimented with different escapements but the verge escapement remained the most popular until the end of the century. Evidently the specialist production of parts and the wholesale manufacturing of movements and cases was very well established indeed by mid-century.

If movements were more or less standardised by 1760, this was certainly not the case with dials. During the 1760-1800 period bracket clocks were made with brass dials with applied brass spandrels and silvered brass chapter rings or plates, though some examples had painted or engraved spandrel corners. Other clocks had plain all-over enamel dials or enamel dials and subsidiary dials set on brass plates with brass, painted or engraved spandrel corners. There were decorated all-over enamel dials in the Battersea tradition, though these were very rare. There were engraved single sheet silvered brass dials. By 1772 painted dials began to appear. There were also clocks which combined painted centres with the traditional applied silvered brass chapter ring. In addition, there were clocks with automata and lunar work, and dials that combined several of the features mentioned. Not all these features were new but it is interesting to note that so many choices of dial and movements, if we include musical and chiming clocks, and choices of case design were being offered at a time when London longcases were being made in fewer numbers with relatively far fewer choices of case and dial design. By contrast, the 1760-1800 period saw a tremendous increase in demand for provincial longcases accompanied by a splendid flowering of different and distinct regional case and dial designs. Provincial bracket clocks, for reasons explained earlier, remained something of a rarity.

The 1760-1800 period was a time of increasing prosperity. Inevitably there was an increasing demand for new good quality furniture. Although the new clocks shared quarters with the new furniture, none of the basic clock case designs can be directly attributed to Sheraton, Chippendale, Hepplewhite or any of the other well-known designers or makers of Georgian furniture, though Gillows, who produced a number of longcase clock cases, appear to have made a tiny handful of Georgian bracket clock cases. Cescinsky and Webster devoted a chapter to the subject in *English Domestic Clocks*. Their two main conclusions were first, that the casework was of less importance and interest than the clock, at least to the clockmaker who commissioned and was the dominant partner in the production of a finished clock. Their second conclusion was that the clock case designs offered in Sheraton's *Cabinet Makers' and Upholsterers' drawing book* and Chippendale's *Director*[1] were in any event unusable and impractical, because the designs[2] would not allow the clocks to function properly. The second conclusion is broadly correct. The first is unfair to the clockmaker, who was certainly not as conservative as Cescinsky and Webster suggest. We have already seen many changes in dial design and a ready acceptance of, for example, Dutch, Chinese and French influences. Equally the casemakers' designs both for the home and export markets are many and varied and must have proved acceptable to the clockmakers who commissioned them.

It is probably true to say that it was difficult for a busy and famous designer or maker of furniture to fit in with working with a clockmaker. Clock cases must perforce conform to the dictates of the shape required to house the dial, movement and pendulum. The specialist cabinet makers who made clock cases were used to working for clockmakers and knew the limitations imposed. They and the clockmakers inhabited a small specialised world which was not easily penetrated by designers and furniture makers, used to working on a larger scale. It is quite clear, however, that clock casemakers were certainly influenced by men such as Sheraton and Chippendale and features ascribed to them or to other famous contemporary designers will often be seen in clock cases. Equally, contemporary trends, the vogue for chinoiserie for example,

1. *English Domestic Clocks*, Cescinsky and Webster.
2. Chippendale and Sheraton clock case designs together with longcase designs based on them are also illustrated and discussed in *Old Clocks and Watches and Their Makers* by F.J. Britten and in *The Longcase Clock*, by T. Robinson. Both published by The Antique Collectors' Club.

PLATE IV/1 *George Sewell.*
Mahogany clock in a case style
popularised by Ellicott. Front
of original bracket slides
forward to form key drawer.
Circa *1765.*

soon appeared in the designs of dial plates and backplates.

But enough of the background to the 1760-1800 period. It is time to look at the bracket clocks themselves.

The clock shown in Plate IV/1 is a mahogany veneered example of the case style introduced by John Ellicott *circa* 1755. The intention was that only that part of the dial needed to show the time would be visible. The earlier example, shown in Plate II/49, retained the applied chapter ring though Ellicott soon realised that an engraved single sheet silvered brass dial, or even a white enamel dial, gave a clearer effect. The idea was copied, the mahogany example in Plate IV/1 was made by George Sewell *circa* 1765. It is an example of a clock that retains its original bracket. As is so often the case, the bottom of the bracket slides forward to provide a drawer for the key.

This Ellicott design can be criticised on the grounds that the ebony examples, with their overpowering black front doors, are rather sombre in appearance.

Plate IV/2 shows an example with an enamel dial. Ellicott's casemaker has here tried to relieve the sombre look by applying brass spandrel corners to the case door. This clock, with its fine rococo feet and rococo mount applied to the inverted bell-top, is undoubtedly a handsome piece but the original clarity and simplicity that Ellicott sought for the design has been completely lost. Nonetheless, the design itself, with or without embellishments, continued to be made until about 1780.

The clock by James Upjohn shown in Plate IV/3 is a great rarity because it is one of very few clocks known that has a genuine decorated enamel dial that gives every appearance of being Battersea enamel. Nine such clocks, four longcases and five bracket clocks, were traced[3] and described and illustrated in a well-researched monograph, 'Faces of Mystery.'[4] Anthony Theelke's researches led him to the conclusion that these painted enamel dials are all the work of Anthony Tregent who was one of three Swiss brothers, two of whom settled in England. Anthony Tregent worked for the Battersea enamel factory before it failed in 1756. It is likely that Tregent foresaw the failure of the Battersea enterprise and accordingly set himself up in business on his own account in Denmark Street, Soho. The clockmakers' dates of manufacturing all fall between 1756 and 1775, so the clock dials are not truly Battersea work but, as they were made by a former Battersea enameller, they have the same status and interest. Anthony Tregent's brother, James, was a well-known London clockmaker, which probably explains why Anthony made some clock dials in addition to other enamel work.

James Upjohn's bell-top clock dates *circa* 1765 and is 17 inches high. It has the usual verge escapement and an engraved backplate. The painted decoration on the enamel dial is a shade of red. The case is of mahogany.

Large decorated enamel on copper dials such as this were difficult and expensive to make and were fragile. Their period of manufacture was limited, due to the fact that painted dials which were easier and cheaper to manufacture started to be made in quantity *circa* 1772. These key factors explain why few large enamel dials are known.

It is surprising that the turntable stands which it is thought were fitted to a number of the earliest seventeenth century bracket clocks went out of favour. The example shown in Plates IV/4 and IV/5 is fitted to a large mahogany musical clock made by John Ellicott *circa* 1765. The movement offers a choice of twelve tunes played at three-hourly intervals. This is a large, heavy clock. Its owner must have been glad of the turntable base when he showed the movement to his friends.

The case at first sight appears to be a wealthy first cousin one generation removed from the transitional clock by John Gordon shown in Plate II/28. But Ellicott's clock is really an elaborate break-arch design to which an inverted

3. Others exist. The writer has seen two more.
4. *Faces of Mystery*, Anthony Theelke.

PLATE IV/2 *Ellicott. Fine brass door mounts enliven sombre appearance but the case and dial lose the clarity originally intended for this design.* Circa *1760.*

PLATE IV/3 *James Upjohn. Mahogany-cased clock with rare example of decorated 'Battersea' enamel dial. Large enamel dials were difficult to make.* Circa *1765.*

bell-top superstructure was added at the time of manufacture to balance the deep moulded turntable base. The design is successful. Plate IV/5 shows the clock full face. The turntable base blends perfectly into the design of the clock.

This is one of very few eighteenth century clocks known with turntable bases. Another example, not illustrated, is a musical clock by William Webster, London. It was exhibited at the Antiquarian Horological Society's Tenth Anniversary Exhibition held at the Science Museum in 1964. The catalogue entry read as follows:

'C. 1740. Musical Spring Clock by William Webster, London. This clock has an eight day movement and an ebonised case in the inverted bell style having flat pilasters on the front with gilt metal mounts and a pierced metal fret below the dome and in the side windows. There is a drawer in the base for the storage of spare pin barrels and the whole stands on a turntable plinth. The dial is break-arch with a pointer for selecting the tunes in the arch and has a mock-pendulum aperture. The fusée movement has three trains with verge escapement and plays a tune every third hour,

PLATE IV/4 *Ellicott. Musical clock showing action of rare turntable base.* Circa *1765.*

PLATE IV/5 *Ellicott's musical turntable clock shown front view.*

there being a selection of eight tunes on each of the three pin-barrels. There is also pull-string quarter repeat on six bells. Height 32½ inches.'

An early eighteenth century turntable clock is illustrated in Colour Plate 11. An early nineteenth century example is shown in Plate VI/9. It will be noted that the use of turntable bases seems to have been restricted to large, heavy clocks.

The thriving export market for English clocks meant that English clockmakers had learned to cater to a wider range of tastes than might have been the case had their efforts been limited to satisfying the home market. Clocks made for export, particularly those for the Turkish and Eastern markets, were often more complex and ornate than the mainstream English production but inevitably there were some English clients who had a taste for such clocks.

Eardley Norton's musical clock, Plate IV/6, is a good example. It is

PLATE IV/6. *Eardley Norton. Ornate tortoiseshell musical clock. Enamel dials set on brass dial plate ornamented with polychrome painted flowers in spandrel corners and Father Time in arch.* Circa 1765.

certainly ornate. The case itself appears to be of tortoiseshell. The gilded brass mounts are exceptional. The basic case design is the bell-top and it is, of course, similar to that shown in Plate II/50. The brass dial plate is painted with Father Time in the arch and is decorated with polychrome painted flowers. The main and subsidiary dials are enamel set onto the painted dial plate. This particular style of case, some later examples of which were fitted with a cupola top, shown in Chapter V, became very popular with export customers and were also made for the home market. The cupola top design was still being used by top London makers during the second half of the nineteenth century.

PLATE IV/7 *William Creak.*
Traditional brass dial but dial
plate, including centre, painted
with a rural scene and flowers.
Circa *1765.*

Eardley Norton was a famous maker who worked from 1760-94. This clock
was made *circa* 1765.

The polychrome painted spandrel corners of Eardley Norton's clock were
not necessarily an export feature. They are painted in a hard, glossy paint
which gives an enamelled effect. The first time the writer saw such a dial
decoration it was assumed that the painted decoration had been applied later,
perhaps in the nineteenth century, but enough examples have now been seen
for it to be certain that this was an occasional design feature on London dials
made between about 1765 and 1780. They are possibly the work of just one

PLATE IV/8 *Edward Pistor.*
Musical clock showing mixture
of features. 'Dutch' minute
bands. French style door
surround. Painted flower
spandrels. Fine brass mounts.
Circa *1770.*

or two studios.

It is clear that enamel dials were the forerunners of the plain painted dials that appeared towards the end of the eighteenth century. Brass dials, decorated with polychrome flowers together with the decorated enamel 'Battersea' dials, should perhaps be seen as the forerunners of the decorated painted dials, both longcase and bracket, that appeared during the same period. But it is extremely unusual to find either a traditional brass bracket or longcase dial whose dial centre contains painted decorations, though painted lunar dials were a common enough feature on brass dial longcase dials. William Creak's mahogany brass dial bracket clock, Plate IV/7, is a rare example. It is 21 ½

PLATE IV/9 *(right) Charles Coulon. Christchurch. Hampshire. Absolutely traditional bell-top clock.* Circa *1770.*

PLATE IV/10 *Justin Vulliamy. A French style case that is clearly a forerunner of the balloon clocks that became fashionable twenty years later.* Circa *1765.*

inches high and was made *circa* 1765. The backplate of the movement, which pull-repeats on six bells, has leafy scroll engraving centred by a basket of flowers. The rococo brass spandrels are absolutely typical of the mid-1760s. The dial centre is painted with an attractive rural scene, whereas the arch is painted with polychrome sprays of summer flowers. William Creak, working 1740-68, was known as a maker of musical clocks. Musical clocks were often made for the Turkish and Eastern markets. The majority of the few painted brass bracket clock dial centres that have been seen have been those on export clocks. It is possible that this was an export feature familiar to Creak and here used for a home-trade clock.

Plate IV/8 shows another example of the polychrome type of dial decoration on a mahogany clock by Edward Pistor, made perhaps ten years later. In this instance, the flowers decorate the centres of the subsidiary chapter rings in the arch as well as the spandrel corners. Edward Pistor's clock is a good example of a clock in which there is, perhaps, a not altogether harmonious blend of features. The inverted bell-top and 'Dutch' wavy minute band would not have been out of place twenty years earlier, nor for that matter the continental influence of the shape of the dial surround. The maker's name is signed on a distinctively shaped plaque fitted behind the dial plate. This is a design that was already in use before 1762. It was used on a bracket clock by the famous Thomas Moore of Ipswich who died in that year. It was very popular by the 1770s. Yet the design of the brass spandrel corners of the front door, the latest

PLATE IV/12 *John Fladgate. Small pad top break-arch clock with brass mounts and unusual double feet. Circa 1760.*

PLATE IV/11 *William Gough. Classic early mahogany clock in inverted bell-top case. The wavy skirting is less common but sometimes seen. Circa 1765.*

feature, suggests a date of *circa* 1770 at the earliest. Edward Pistor's clock is musical with a three train bell-striking movement playing one of twelve tunes on the hour on sixteen bells with twenty-seven hammers. It is 25½ inches high without the feet, which are missing. Edward Pistor was working 1755-90. He was succeeded by his sons.

Plate IV/9, by contrast, shows an absolutely standard traditional bell-top clock, *circa* 1770, by Charles Coulon of Christchurch, in which all the features are contemporary and blend well together. A Charles Coulon, probably the same man, is listed as a clockmaker and wine merchant in London, 1743-68. Perhaps he moved to Christchurch, Hampshire. Intriguingly, a Coulon, no Christian name given, is listed in Geneva in 1780. Possibly Charles Coulon was Swiss by origin and eventually returned to Switzerland.

Justin Vulliamy was a famous maker. He too came originally from Switzerland and worked until *circa* 1790. He is well-known for the elegant simplicity that characterised many of his longcase and bracket clocks. A typical example is shown in Colour Plate 15. The *circa* 1765 example shown now in Plate IV/10 is not, in the writer's view, a particularly attractive clock but is certainly not without interest because it is clearly a forerunner of the balloon clock. Vulliamy's clock is very French in style and feeling and is clearly based on a French design of 1703 by Daniel Marot.[5] The earliest form of balloon, see Plate IV/95, derives from it. We can safely say the balloon style is of French origin but the final form, clocks in the style of Plate IV/96, if seen in isolation, do not betray their French origins. They have become completely anglicised and Sheraton in feeling.

The 1750-75 period was, as suggested earlier, a time of great experimentation with clock cases and dial designs. Ellicott's simple square door round dial design (Plates II/49, II/54) and typical early mahogany classic inverted bell-top designs, such as the *circa* 1765 example by William Gough shown in in Plate IV/11, coexisted with the Eardley Norton and Vulliamy designs just shown. Even the classic break-arch case design such as that made by Justin Vulliamy and his father-in-law, Benjamin Gray, during their 1743-62 partnership, Colour Plate 13, did not escape attention, as can be seen if it is compared with the *circa* 1760 example by John Fladgate, Plate IV/12. Bracket clock cases with pillars are usually large but this example, with its unusual double feet, is only 15 inches high. The five pillar movement pull-repeats on six bells. In the writer's opinion the double feet and pillars do not improve upon the original design.

John Roberts' clock, Plate IV/13, shows another attempt to improve upon the classic break-arch. John Roberts, working 1756-90 in St. James's market, was a maker whose clocks are very varied in appearance, compare this example made *circa* 1765 with the clock shown in Plate IV/33. The Roberts' clock in Plate IV/13 makes much use of brass mounts. The dial is fairly conventional.

The three train musical clock, Plate IV/14, by Wagstaffe of London is a case with a curious mix of styles. It was made *circa* 1770 and houses a tune selection lever in the painted dial arch. Possibly the arch once also contained automata. The spandrel corners contain painted polychrome flowers. The dial is of

5. Daniel Marot, *Nouveaux Livre d'Ornements*, 1703, 1713. Illustrated page 438 of *Pictorial Dictionary of British 18th Century Furniture Design*, compiled by Elizabeth White.

PLATE IV/13 *John Roberts. Walnut break-arch clock with fine rococo brass mounts and double feet. An attempt at improving the basic break-arch design.* Circa *1760.*

PLATE IV/14 *(left) Wagstaffe. Large musical clock with rococo mounts. The mahogany case with perhaps an unhappy mix of styles. Enamel dial. Painted polychrome spandrel corners. Circa 1770.*

PLATE IV/15 *(below left) James Cowan. Edinburgh. A timepiece whose mahogany case exhibits Chippendale features. Circa 1770.*

PLATE IV/16 *John Ellicott. A clock in which the bracket forms an integral part of the clock case. The upper part slides forward in the manner of a longcase hood to reveal the movement. Circa 1765.*

enamel. The proportions of the case are perhaps not improved by the clumsy-looking superstructure.

This activity among the case designers was not limited to London. Plate IV/15 shows a mahogany bracket clock *circa* 1770 by James Cowan, a well-known Edinburgh maker who had worked with the famous Julien Leroy in Paris. The case of Cowan's clock, with its applied fretting, exhibits Chippendale features. Yet the dial and front door design are clearly based on Ellicott's design. The clock is a timepiece only. James Cowan was apprenticed in 1744 and died in 1781.

Colour Plate 12 shows a fine large quarter-chiming clock made *circa* 1770 by Conyers Dunlop. This clock has lunar work. The four case corner pillars, reminiscent of longcase hood pillars of the period, are completely in proportion and add to the graceful appearance of the clock.

At some time in the late 1750s or early 1760s, an attempt was made to popularise bracket clocks in which the bracket formed an integral part of the clock case. The example by John Ellicott, Plate IV/16, is typical of the 1765 period. The earliest examples had applied chapter rings and spandrels. The movements of these clocks are mounted on the bracket from which the whole of the upper part of the case can be slid forward. These clocks are graceful in appearance but were perhaps not considered as versatile as the usual bracket clock. A small number were made, invariably by top-flight makers, during the period 1755-80. It has been suggested that they alone can be considered to be bracket clocks. If this view is accepted then this book is too long!

An interesting variation of the arch dial is shown in Plate IV/17. The case is the familiar bell-top with well pronounced female terms. The movement is three train and was made *circa* 1765 by Stephen Rimbault. There are automata in the arch which may have been painted by Zoffany (See Chapter II). A very similar clock by Thomas Moore of Ipswich, made *circa* 1760, is illustrated in Haggar and Miller's *Suffolk Clocks and Clockmakers*. This particular dial shape is well suited to dials with twin subsidiaries such as the 'World Time' example shown in Plate IV/18. This clock was made *circa* 1770 by James Tregent, brother of Anthony Tregent the enameller, already referred to. It is quarter chiming on eight bells. The hour hands are attached to a central boss and move together. They show the time in six different capitals. This is not a feature which could have been useful in the pre-telegraph, pre-telephone era. Nonetheless, this is an interesting forerunner of the 'World Time' clocks seen in the offices of international companies today. The twin subsidiaries are for strike/silent and rise and fall regulation. The dial plates are enamel.

Colour Plate 14 shows a third, entirely conventional, example of this style in a fine, brass mounted, mahogany case. This three train musical clock was made *circa* 1770 by Eardley Norton. Both these clocks have carrying handles fitted to the sides of their cases.

Colour Plate 15 illustrates a type of case which was much used by Justin Vulliamy. It is ebonised. It will be seen that it is a variation of the normal inverted bell-top. The bell-top is flattened to give it the same depth as the low wide arch. This clock dates *circa* 1775.

PLATE IV/17 *Stephen Rimbault. Quarter chiming clock with automata. This variation of the arch dial started to appear* circa *1760.*

Reference has already been made to the impracticality of Chippendale bracket clock designs. A Scottish bracket clock with Chippendale features has already been described and illustrated, but in Plate IV/20 a mahogany bracket clock is shown which derives directly from Chippendale's 'Director', though it owes more perhaps to the longcase designs illustrated than to the bracket clocks. The maker, John MacFarlan, is not listed by either Baillie, Britten or Loomes. There is no place name given on the plaque which bears his name.

PLATE IV/18 *James Tregent. An early example of a 'World Time' dial. The six hour hands show the time in various capitals.* Circa *1770.*

PLATE IV/19 *(facing page) Vulliamy. The movement of a musical clock by this well known maker.*

PLATE IV/20 *John MacFarlan. Scotland. A Chippendale style case of a type that was made by a few Scottish makers.* Circa *1770.*

The applied spandrel corners are of a type that is sometimes found on provincial Scottish longcases of the period. The dial centre, engraved against a matted background, is of a style found on longcase dials mid-century in the Midlands and north of England and as late as 1780 in Scotland. The clock probably dates *circa* 1770, i.e. from about the same period as the virtually identically cased clock illustrated by Britten[6] made by the James Cowan of Edinburgh already mentioned.

The 'Chinese Chippendale' look, here exemplified by the pagoda top, clearly found favour with some Scottish bracket clockmakers, yet although a modified pagoda top is common on London and some provincial longcases of the period, it was not adopted for London or provincial English bracket clock cases. Chinoiserie designs for backplates and even dials, however, became extremely popular on English bracket clocks. Plate IV/21 shows an excellent example of a silvered dial plate by Abel Panchaud dating *circa* 1775. Plate

6. *Old Clocks and Watches and Their Makers*, F.J. Britten. Antique Collectors' Club edition. Page 393. Figure 759.

PLATE IV/21 *Abel Panchaud. An example of the popular chinoiserie decoration applied to a dial plate.* Circa *1775.*

PLATE IV/22 *Unsigned. Probably provincial. Chinoiserie decoration applied to a backplate.* Circa *1775.*

IV/22 shows the backplate of an unsigned provincial clock probably of the same period. Plate IV/23 shows the backplate of a bracket clock, *circa* 1775, by Henry Sanderson of London. Henry Sanderson's clock is a classic, good mahogany clock of the period, as can be seen in Plate IV/38.

The last twenty-five years or so of the eighteenth century was a period of consolidation in the manufacture of bracket clocks following the transitional and gestatory period referred to at the beginning of this chapter. Even so, there were so many innovations and detail changes within the broader concept that it is practical to divide the rest of this chapter into four sections, namely, Painted dial clocks, Bell-top clocks, Break-arch clocks and Balloon clocks.

It is hoped that this division will give a clearer perspective of the detail changes as they affected the clocks in each of the sections mentioned. Obviously, many of the case fittings and dial details were common to clocks in different sections. For example, diamond pattern matching brass hands could occur on clocks in any section during their appropriate period, i.e. from about 1790-1810. It should be remembered, however, that there was also considerable overlapping of features. For example, an all-over silvered dial

PLATE IV/23 *Henry Sanderson. Typical chinoiserie backplate of a London clock. (Front view of this clock is Plate IV/38.)* Circa *1780.*

PLATE IV/24 *Abel Panchaud. Typical bell-top mahogany clock. The dial shown in greater detail in Plate IV/21.* Circa *1775.*

could have been used in 1760, 1800 or 1830. The writer has, of course, attempted to point to other features of each of the clocks shown, in order to suggest a reasonably accurate date of manufacture. The fact that a good run of clocks is shown in each category, more or less in chronological order, should also be of help.

Painted Dial Clocks 1772-1800

On the 28 September 1772 the *Birmingham Gazette* carried an advertisement which is thought to be the earliest advertisement for painted dials:[7]

'White clock Dials
Osborn and Wilson, manufacturers of White Clocks
Dials in imitation of Enamel, in a Manner entirely new, have opened a Warehouse at No. 3, in Colmore-Row, Birmingham, where they have an Assortment of the above mentioned Goods. Those who favour them with their Orders may depend upon their being executed with the utmost Punctuality and Expedition.

N.B. The dial Feet will be rivetted to the Dials and such methods used as will enable the Clock Makers to fix them to the Movements.'

7. Reprinted from *White Dial Clocks*, Brian Loomes. Brian Loomes was responsible for the original research on this subject and for bringing white dial longcases to the attention of the public.

The painted dials were an immediate success. Soon there were many painted dial manufacturers at work in Birmingham and other industrial centres. Interestingly, the painted dials had their greatest success in the Midlands and north. By 1800 longcases with painted dials were the norm there, though some makers and their clients still preferred clocks with traditional brass dials with chapter rings and spandrels, or all-over silvered and engraved brass dials. Longcase clocks with painted dials were sold before 1800 in the south but in far smaller numbers. They were very rare indeed on London longcase clocks pre-1800.

The dial plates of painted dial longcase clocks were invariably made from rolled sheet iron, both sides of which were thickly coated with a brown primer. The show side was then painted white to give the background colour. It is thought that the painted dial plate was usually heated or baked at this stage to harden the paint surface. To enable the clockmaker to position the clock on the movement more easily, the dial feet were often fitted to a falseplate. The clockmaker would make short brass feet to attach his movement to the falseplate.

Falseplates had already been used, and continued in use, with convex enamel bracket clock dials. They were attached to the fragile enamel dial, which was fired onto copper, either by pinned lugs attached to the back of the enamel dial or by a central retaining collet. In this case steady pins were fitted to the circumference of the falseplate, which lined up with notches in the circumference of the enamel dial. Occasionally the dial was attached to the falseplate by screws. This appears to be the case with the moulded Battersea enamel arch dial shown in Plate IV/3. Indeed, a large fragile dial of this type would always have been fitted to a strong falseplate, but pinned lugs were usually used to secure enamel dials and enamel subsidiary dials onto brass dial plates such as that of the Vulliamy clock illustrated in Colour Plate 15. Convex painted dials were attached to falseplates using the same methods, save that the writer cannnot recall seeing screws used. When flat painted dials were attached to a brass dial plate to give an effect similar to that given by the enamel dials mounted on a brass plate then, once again, pinned lugs were used.

Flat painted bracket clock dials, whatever their shape, though at this period these were usually arched, were identical in form to the contemporary all-over silvered and engraved brass dials, save that instead of being silvered and engraved the brass dial plate was painted. The paint did not always key particularly well to the brass and some painted dial plates were accordingly made of tinned iron, which provided better adhesion for the paint.

During the last thirty years of the Georgian period, 1800-30, painted dials were the commonest type of dial fitted to bracket clocks but during the 1772-1800 period they were not particularly common. They were considered as an alternative type of dial. It is also true that they were not considered to be a cheaper form of dial than the brass dial. They were fitted to movements of the same quality contained in cases of the same quality as the contemporary brass dial bracket clock. They were, however, obviously cheaper and much easier to make than the expensive enamel dials they so closely resembled.

Enamel dials had always been difficult to make in larger sizes and were very fragile. No doubt this was why they were often mounted on brass dial plates.

Painted dials had the same advantages as enamel dials, namely clarity and legibility, in an age when houses were ill-lit. It was for this reason, of course, that brass chapter rings had always been silvered. B. Loomes, in *White Dial Clocks*, suggests that the decorated painted dials brought a touch of the beauty and colour of nature into the home. No doubt lacquer clocks and furniture, much brighter when newly made, enjoyed their long run of popularity for the same reason.

There is a definite progression in the design of the decoration of painted dial longcase clocks that allows a knowledgeable person to date fairly accurately examples made between 1772 and about 1850. Obviously some styles overlap and recur but an estimate within ten years can usually be made. B. Loomes, the foremost authority on painted dial longcase clocks, is of the opinion that there is less visible progression and much more overlapping of these features on arch painted dial bracket clocks of the 1772-1800 period, first because London makers showed a marked preference for the plain white dial, probably because it looked like an enamel dial, an expensive product with which their customers were already familiar, and second because so few provincial bracket clocks were sold. The total number of early painted dial bracket clocks that would have had flower or otherwise decorated corners and other colour contrast features was thus limited to the very few London clocks whose dials are so decorated and, remembering the much smaller demand for bracket clocks in the provinces, an equally small number of early provincial examples. Given such a small and widespread sample, it is not surprising that no particular progression is discernible between 1772 and 1800. In any event, painted bracket clock dials were themselves new and any feature introduced during this period must have appeared innovatory to the general public. As we know, the manufacture of decorated white painted dials started in the Midlands and spread to the north. Birmingham and the Midlands from the start had an available workforce of people with the necessary skills required to make, paint and decorate these dials.

The Midlands and north always provided the greatest demand for decorated painted longcase dials though eventually, of course, there were decorated painted dial manufacturers in the south and west too. But London was never seriously in the market for decorated white painted dials either during the late eighteenth century or during the 1800-30 period. London bracket clockmakers preferred a plain white dial throughout the relevant later Georgian period and London longcases progressed from all-over silvered and engraved brass dials direct to plain white painted dials. Decorated white painted dials are virtually never seen on London longcases. Plain white painted dials were, of course, easy to produce and were certainly made in London for the London bracket clock market and eventually for longcases. But the early London painted bracket clock dials that are decorated in the manner of contemporary provincial longcase painted dials almost certainly had dials that were ordered from Birmingham.

PLATE IV/25 *Edward Tutet. Alarum bracket clock. The decorated painted dial probably made in Birmingham. Circa 1790.*

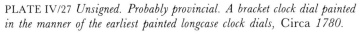

PLATE IV/26 *Robert Kelvey. Gainsborough. Ebonised bell-top clock with decorated painted dial reminiscent of contemporary painted longcase dials.* Circa *1785.*

PLATE IV/27 *Unsigned. Probably provincial. A bracket clock dial painted in the manner of the earliest painted longcase clock dials, Circa 1780.*

Colour Plate 16 shows a fine mahogany inverted bell-top bracket clock made *circa* 1790. The full arch painted dial is signed Thos. Hunter London. This is a good example of a decorated white painted dial. It is, of course, very Birmingham in appearance and closely resembles the contemporary decorated white painted longcase dials. This clock retains the verge escapement and engraved backplate that would have been the norm had it been made, as might easily have been the case, with the all-over silvered and engraved brass dial that is also well suited to the full arch dial shape. Plate IV/25 shows another example made *circa* 1790 by Edward Tutet of London. This dial too shows all the Birmingham features. The maker's name on this dial has been restored at some time and has been misspelt Tatet. Plate IV/26 shows a good provincial clock *circa* 1785 by Robert Kelvey of Gainsborough. Once more there can be little doubt that the dial was provincially made, though it would have been perfectly possible for the clockmaker to have ordered the movement, and perhaps even the ebonised pearwood bell-top case, from trade sources in London. This clock too originally had a verge escapement.

In Plate IV/27 the dial from an unsigned, probably provincial mahogany break-arch painted dial bracket clock is shown. This is a dial design that continued in use until about 1800. It is interesting because it exactly copies the design of the earliest painted longcase clock dials made *circa* 1775. The spandrel corners were painted with a raised and gilded design that clearly imitated the rococo brass spandrels of the contemporary brass dial longcases.

Plates IV/28 and IV/29 illustrate a good quality London break-arch mahogany clock that is absolutely typical of the plain painted dial clocks made in the capital between about 1785 and 1805. The maker is Benjamin Simkin, who was working 1781-1807. The well engraved backplate retains the usual verge backcock, though because the clock is fitted with rise and fall regulation the pendulum is suspended outside the backcock. This arrangement is quite common at this period, particularly, it is noted, on painted dial clocks. It suggests that a standard movement, probably held in stock unfinished by a wholesale manufacturer, was ordered to be finished to suit the client, who in this instance specified rise and fall pendulum regulation. The elegant mahogany case, with its brass-bound pad top and brass fish-scale side frets, could, of course, just as easily have housed a brass dial clock.

Geometric corner decorations and arabic hour numbers are features normally associated with the painted dials on longcases made 1800-20 but here, Plate IV/30, they are used on a painted dial bracket clock that was probably made in the 1795-99 period, because it is signed simply 'Chaplin. Bury'. The Chaplin brothers were in partnership together from 1776-99. William Chaplin died in 1799. This is another good provincial example whose dial probably originated in Birmingham.

Daniel De Saint Leu was a very fine maker who made a number of important clocks. The dial of the large three train musical clock shown in Plate IV/31 is, of course, painted, though it has been incorrectly restored at some time and the maker's name misspelt. But the painted dial confirms the point that painted dials were not considered to be a cheaper type. It would have been

COLOUR PLATE 13 *(above) Justin Vulliamy and Benjamin Gray. Classic break-arch ebonised case with three pad top.* Circa *1760.*

COLOUR PLATE 12 *(left) Conyers Dunlop. A large quarter chiming mahogany clock with lunar dial.* Circa *1770.*

PLATE IV/28 *(left) Benjamin Simkin. Undecorated plain white painted dials were preferred by London makers.* Circa *1785.*

PLATE IV/29 *Benjamin Simkin. The backplate of the clock shown in Plate IV/28. The rise and fall adjustable pendulum mounted outside the verge backcock.*

impractical to make an enamel dial of this size (the dial plate is 8 inches wide) but a silvered engraved brass dial would have been perfectly fashionable and acceptable when this very costly clock was made *circa* 1795. The musical work and backplate are shown in Colour Plate 17. The clock has verge escapement and stands 24 inches high.

Plate IV/32 shows an example of a clock with a 6¾ inch brass dial plate which is fitted with a painted chapter plate and subsidiary dial. The maker's name, originally painted on the dial, has now been lost. This is a good quality mahogany bracket clock, originally with verge escapement. The backplate is engraved with flowers and leaves around a basket of fruit. The case is of well-figured mahogany and stands 19 inches high.

Bell-top Bracket Clocks 1775-1800

The first clock in this series, a true bell-top clock made *circa* 1770 by John Roberts of London, Plate IV/33, is discussed now because it forms a good link

PLATE IV/30 *Chaplin. Bury St. Edmunds. Suffolk. Decorated painted dial with geometric corners and Arabic numerals. Dials like this were commmonly used on painted dial longcases 1800-30. This early example is* circa *1795.*

PLATE IV/31 *(below left) Daniel De Saint Leu. Painted dials were not considered inferior. Painted dial here used on an expensive mahogany-cased musical clock. Circa 1795.*

PLATE IV/32 *Unsigned. Probably London. Painted dials, as an alternative to enamel, were sometimes mounted on brass dial plates. Circa 1785.*

COLOUR PLATE 14 *Eardley Norton. Musical mahogany bell-top clock with flattened arch dial. Circa 1770.*

COLOUR PLATE 15 *Justin Vulliamy. Ebonised shallow break-arch case of a design much favoured by this maker.* Circa *1775.*

PLATE IV/33 *John Roberts. Large quarter chiming ebonised bell-top bracket clock whose door and dial show a mixture of Dutch, French, English and English provincial features.* Circa *1770.*

PLATE IV/34 *Joseph Smith. Bristol. Well-balanced quarter chiming bell-top clock with lunar and tidal dial.* Circa *1770.*

between the transitional gestatory period referred to at the beginning of this chapter and the clocks of the 1775-1800 period.

The ebonised case of the John Roberts clock, with its fine brass mounts and acanthus feet, is absolutely in keeping with the 1775-1800 period but the dial is beginning to look a little old fashioned. The pierced centres of the subsidiary dials are attractive, but this is a feature we found mid-century and earlier. The dotted decoration round the winding holes looks rather provincial. The pie-crust border of the date dial is a feature usually seen bordering the seconds dials of some country longcases made *circa* 1770 or earlier. The 'Dutch' wavy minute band is a feature which was at its most popular some fifteen years earlier but the case door corner spandrels and general 'feel' of the case still bring us back to the *circa* 1770 date. If this clock is compared with the earlier clock shown by John Roberts (Plate IV/13) one is left with the impression that here we have a maker who sought variety in his work but sometimes lacked the ability to plan a successful blend of different styles and periods. The clock is 23½ inches high and is quarter chiming on eight bells.

PLATE IV/35 *John Waldron.*
Conventional quarter chiming
mahogany bell-top clock typical
of its period. Circa *1775.*

Joseph Smith of Bristol's clock, Plate IV/34, presents an altogether more balanced appearance. This too is a clock made *circa* 1770 but nearly all the features, case, spandrels, hands, matted dial centre, painted lunar phase (it also shows the state of the tide, presumably at Bristol), are what you would expect at this time. The only features which are becoming, perhaps, a little old fashioned by 1770 are the pad feet. The clock stands 24 inches high. The backplate is engraved with leafy scrolls and flowers.

John Waldron of Cornhill, London was the maker of the particularly good-looking quarter-chiming clock shown in Plate IV/35. The case is of well-figured mahogany and stands about 17 inches high. The design of the hands, the fine brass frets, the pad feet and the rococo spandrels have all been seen on clocks made earlier which suggests a date for this clock of nearer 1770 than 1780, but the whole clock is well-planned and of excellent appearance.

Normand McPherson of Edinburgh worked from 1759-83. He was the

PLATE IV/36 *Normand McPherson. Edinburgh. Ebonised bell-top clock indistinguishable from a London clock but undoubtedly made in Edinburgh.* Circa *1775.*

PLATE IV/37 *Interesting and well-engraved backplate of Normand McPherson's clock.*

PLATE IV/38 *Henry Sanderson. Mahogany inverted bell-top case. Particularly well-balanced dial.* Circa *1780.*

nephew of a Scottish chief, which may have been of some help to him. He certainly built up an extensive business.[8] The ebonised clock shown in Plate IV/36 is well-proportioned and stands some 17 inches high. This is a difficult clock to date. The general look of the clock suggests *circa* 1775 but the earlier style rococo case corner spandrels could infer a date of a few years earlier. A handsome Scottish-made clock clearly based on the London examples. Plate IV/37 shows the unusual and well-engraved backplate.

The inverted bell-top continued in use until the end of the eighteenth century. Plate IV/38 shows a particularly good example standing 17 inches high. This clock was made by Henry Sanderson of the Strand, London. This is a clock in which great care has been taken to make a pleasing blend of all the constituents. The design of the plaque bearing the maker's name, the hands, the spandrels and case corner spandrels are all in harmony. The case is of well-figured mahogany.

The clock by William Turnbull of Darlington, Plates IV/39 and IV/40, is of particular interest because as well as being fitted with pull-quarter repeating work it also has rise and fall regulation, a backplate signed by the engraver in addition to the maker, and original anchor escapement. This is only the second bracket clock seen by the writer which bears the engraver's signature. The other is on the backplate of the Burtt Wade break-arch bracket clock *circa* 1770 shown in Plate IV/66. The excellent rococo engraving on the backplate of Turnbull's clock still contains strapwork, a rather old fashioned feature on a clock made *circa* 1775. The pendulum for the anchor escapement is suspended from a vertically extending backcock, the rise and fall of which is controlled by a vertical rack and pinion. This is a very early example of anchor escapement on a bracket clock, though by about 1800 anchor escapements were common enough. Eventually, of course, they replaced the verge but the writer has not infrequently seen original verge escapements in early nineteenth century bracket clocks. William Turnbull is listed working from 1761-80.

It had long been appreciated that brass mounts went well with black bracket clocks. Walnut bracket clocks were more usually not originally fitted with brass mounts. But that is certainly not the case with mahogany bracket clocks. John Miles[9] of Stroud's clock, Plate IV/41, is very small, the height to the top of the case being only 12 inches. The very fine brass mounts were obviously made specially for this clock. All-over silvered dials were in use relatively early in the Gloucestershire[10] area. A longcase has been seen by William Mills of Tetbury with a movement dated 1771. The dial is silvered and engraved. John Miles was a well-known Stroud maker who was working 1773-86. He probably made this clock *circa* 1780.

When the writer first saw John Miles' clock it was fitted with a lever escapement in order that it could be used on a yacht. Subsequently the verge escapement was put back. A handful of bracket clocks were made for travelling which were fitted with verge escapement controlled by a balance wheel as well as the usual pendulum so that a choice could be made. The most famous example was that made by Tompion in 1693. Later, in the nineteenth century, numbers of high quality English carriage, or four glass clocks as they are

8. *Old Scottish Clockmakers*, John Smith.
9. John Miles' work is discussed in *Gloucestershire Clocks and Watchmakers*, Graham Dowler.
10. Andrew Nicholls in *English Bracket and Mantel Clocks* describes and illustrates a provincial inverted bell-top mahogany bracket clock with reeded and canted corners, stopped with brass, with a square silvered brass dial by Henry Stimpson, Bath, who died in 1766.

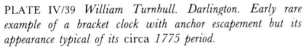

PLATE IV/39 *William Turnbull. Darlington. Early rare example of a bracket clock with anchor escapement but its appearance typical of its* circa 1775 *period.*

PLATE IV/40 *Backplate showing original anchor pendulum of Turnbull's clock and backplate signed by the engraver.*

PLATE IV/41 *John Miles. Stroud. Small mahogany bell-top clock with silvered dial and exceptional brass mounts. Circa 1780.*

PLATE IV/42 *(facing page) George Prior. Mahogany bell-top clock with exceptional brass mounts. Mounts were often gilded.*

PLATE IV/43 *John Green. A quarter chiming clock, the dial centre of which is left unmatted and was probably originally silvered.* Circa *1775.*

PLATE IV/44 *Robert Clark. A later example of a clock with an applied chapter ring in which the dial centre is left unmatted. The case design of this clock is fairly simple.* Circa *1785.*

sometimes known, were made with lever escapements.

The handsome quarter striking mahogany clock by George Prior, Plate IV/42, is another clock of about the same period. It too is fitted with very fine brass mounts. Mounts of this quality were often gilded. The fine rococo spandrels of the clock are similar to the spandrel corners of the front doors of a number of clocks already illustrated.

A variation in dial design that occurs occasionally from about 1775 onwards is that the centre of the dial of clocks fitted with the traditional chapter ring and spandrels is left plain, rather than being matted. This feature can be found on clocks made as late as about 1800, see Plate IV/91. Plate IV/43 shows an example by John Green, St. Martin's Court (London) made *circa* 1775. This is a quarter chiming clock in a good mahogany case. Plate IV/44 shows a later example in a simpler mahogany case without canted or decorated case corners by Robert Clark, London. It was made *circa* 1785.

Plate IV/47 illustrates the difficulty that can sometimes occur in dating a bracket clock. Here is an ebonised bell-top clock by William Phipps of Evesham for whom we have only one date, *circa* 1785 (Loomes). But William

PLATE IV/45 *William Vale. A simple timepiece, right hand winding hole is only for appearance. Lightly engraved dial centre. Plain ebonised bell-top case.* Circa 1785.

PLATE IV/46 *The movement with tapered plates of William Vale's clock. Action of verge escapement can be seen clearly.*

Phipps' clock, a handsome piece, has no early or late features for a clock of its supposed period. All we can say is that it is unlikely to have been made before about 1775 or after about 1790. The backplate, Plate IV/48, gives three clues. First there is an engraved basket of plenty, fashionable from the early days until virtually the end of the eighteenth century. Second, the plates are footed, sometimes, but by no means invariably, a feature found on clocks made in the last twenty years of the century or later. Lastly, there is the figure '2515' engraved top right on the backplate. This could be a Thwaites number but if this were so we would arrive at an approximate date of *circa* 1801, which seems too late. It could be that William Phipps numbered his jobs or his clocks, though if he made 2515 clocks we should surely know more of him. It could be the number of a wholesale trade manufacturer other than J. Thwaites, such as William Robson of London, though the Robson movements seen by the writer have not been numbered.

It is worth making the point that the record books are by no means infallible. The information contained in them is the sum total of details originating from

PLATE IV/47 *William Phipps. Evesham. Typical good provincial clock with unusual spandrels.* Circa *1780.*

PLATE IV/48 *Backplate of William Phipps of Evesham's clock.*

many different sources. For example, apparent working dates may be taken from trade directories. If a maker stopped his subscription in, say, 1780 he may be shown 1760-80, yet he may have worked for another ten years. Sometimes a single date refers to a lost watch newspaper advertisement date. It may also be a date of birth, or death, or just a guess provided by the owner of a clock by a previously unrecorded maker. Many of the makers recorded by Britten are not recorded by Baillie and vice versa. And although Loomes, a trained genealogist, updated and added to Britten and Baillie, he too was dependent on information from a multitude of sources. The reference books include the membership dates of men who were members of the Clockmakers' Company. There are other published sources such as the several regional clockmaking books. Surprisingly, there are still many unrecorded makers.

To summarise. Details of makers can be looked for first in all the reference books, the writer normally travels with at least a dozen, but in the absence of information or the presence of what is thought to be inaccurate information, you should make your own judgement using your own eyes, knowledge and instincts or ask someone you believe to be knowledgeable. Interestingly, a well-known dealer, asked to date William Phipps' clock, unhesitatingly suggested *circa* 1780, a date with which the writer concurs.

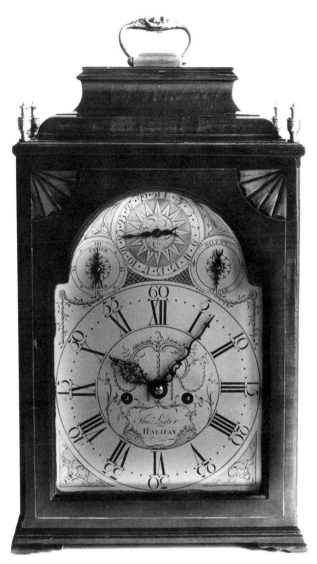

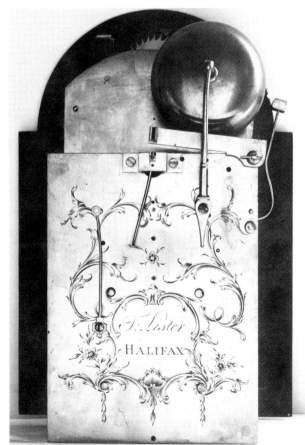

PLATE IV/49 *Thomas Lister II. Halifax. Highly individual provincial inverted bell-top clock. Sheraton style corner inlays to case. Heavily engraved dial. Circa 1790.*

PLATE IV/50 *Movement of Thomas Lister's clock. The pinwheel escapement was sometimes used by this maker. Ting-tang quarter striking. (Quarter hammers and bells missing.)*

PLATE IV/51 *Backplate of Thomas Lister's clock.*

PLATE IV/52 *(Right) Chancellor. A London-made inverted bell-top mahogany-cased clock with Sheraton style fan inlays. A variation of the Ellicott square door round dial design shown in Plate II/49. Arabic numerals. Circa 1795.*

PLATE IV/53 *(Below right) Ellicott. Musical clock whose movement was made, as were many musical movements, by Thwaites. Circa 1780.*

PLATE IV/54 *(Below) Benjamin Pyke. Heavily decorated cases were often used for large musical clocks. Well-engraved silvered dial plate. Circa 1775.*

The Listers were a famous Yorkshire family of clockmakers who worked from about 1715 until the last of them, Thomas Lister II of Halifax, died in 1814. Thomas Lister II was the maker of the interesting clock shown in Plate IV/49. He was a particularly ingenious man. In addition to ordinary clocks he made musical and world-time clocks. The inverted bell-top case of this example owes little to London. Even the handle is of a pattern not usually seen. The Sheraton-style fan inlays in the corners of the front door of the mahogany case are of box or holly. The centre of the dial plate is engraved. The centres of London all-over silvered dial clocks of this period tend to be left plain save for the maker's name. The spandrel corners are engraved following the style of painted dial corners of the period. The arch is used for a day-of-the-month dial, rise and fall regulation and strike/silent. The minutes are shown by dots. Dotted minutes are a feature of provincial longcases, particularly in the north-west, during the 1785-95 period. They can sometimes be found on bracket clocks both in London and the provinces.

Plate IV/50 shows the pin-wheel escapement of Thomas Lister's clock. The pin barrel, visible top right between the plates, drives the bell hammers of the ting-tang quarter striking. The two hammers and the two smaller quarter bells were missing when this photograph was taken. Ting-tang quarter striking is a feature often found in nineteenth century continental clocks. English makers usually fitted a third train when quarter striking was required but just occasionally a two train English longcase or bracket clock will be found that ting-tang quarter strikes from two trains. A painted dial musical bracket clock made by Thomas Lister II is also fitted with pin-wheel escapement. The pin wheel escapement was commonly used on the continent but is a rare feature on English clocks. Another clock by this maker, a longcase, had all the days of the year divided into the months engraved around the circumference of the dial. The calendar hand revolved once during the year. The advantage of this system was that there was no need to make a correction for months of less than thirty-one days. It was, of course, necessary to adjust the hand on leap years.

Plates IV/53 and IV/54 show two musical clocks by Ellicott and Benjamin Pyke respectively. The cases are similar, inasmuch as both are of the heavily decorated variety of bell-top that often seems to have been used for large musical clocks, but Pyke's clock has a full arch top to the dial and a French-style waisted dial surround. The full arch is usually an end of the century feature, as is the decorated bezel, but the steel hands of the pattern fitted are not seen as often towards the end of the century as the diamond pattern fitted to Ellicott's clock. Very often these diamond pattern hands are gilded or of polished brass. They started to become popular *circa* 1790 but the brass version was probably already being used with enamel or white painted dials a few years earlier. The movement of Ellicott's clock, like many late eighteenth and early nineteenth century musical movements, was made by Thwaites, who supplied a large number of movements of all sorts to Ellicott. It bears the Thwaites number 361. Buggins and Turner gives approximate dates for Thwaites' numbers[11] but Thwaites' output could only be estimated before 1780. Conjecturally number 361 could have been made as early as 1768 or as late

11. A useful and easily available dating chart of J. Thwaites and Thwaites and Reed numbers is given in *English Dial Clocks* by Ronald Rose. The numbers correspond with the chart given by Buggins and Turner in *Antiquarian Horology*, September 1973. Their article, 'The Context of Production, Identification and Dating of clocks by A. and J. Thwaites', gives much background information about the London clock trade. Thwaites and Reed records are held at the Guildhall Library, London. Another assessment of Thwaites numbers, 1788-1801 is given by Adrian Burchall, *Antiquarian Horology*, September 1982, page 461.

PLATE IV/55 *Thomas Chantler. Full arch dial quarter chiming clock showing seconds in the arch. Circa 1790.*

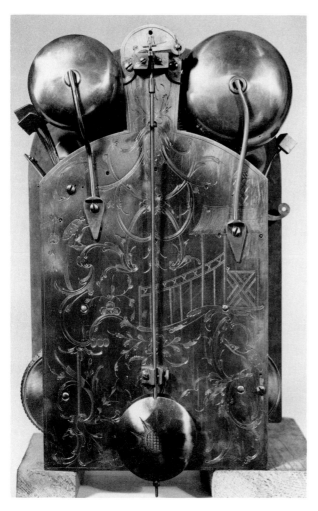

PLATE IV/56 *Unusual tic-tac escapement of Chantler's clock.*

PLATE IV/57 *(left) Shaped backplate with chinoiserie engraving of Chantler's clock.*

PLATE IV/58 *Thomas Chantler. A more conventional clock. Large solid spandrels are a sometimes seen variation used in conjunction with enamel dial plates. Circa 1790.*

PLATE IV/59 *Brothers Melly and Martin. Applied silvered brass chapter plates are another variation of contemporary dial design. Circa 1795.*

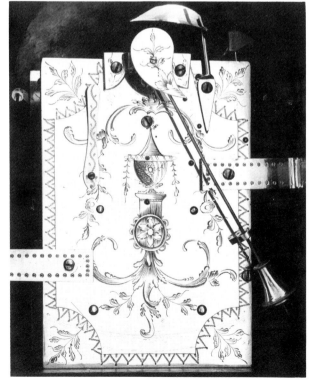

PLATE IV/60 *The backplate of the Brothers Melly and Martin's clock.*

PLATE IV/61 *Haley & Son. Silvering solutions of the period gave an almost white effect. It could be difficult to distinguish between silvered, painted or enamel dials. This dial is silvered brass.* Circa *1790.*

PLATE IV/62 *Henry Bell. Lancaster. Typical silvered dial engraving of its period. Elegant but simpler bell-top case.* Circa *1790.*

as 1780. If the clock is dated *circa* 1780 then the brass diamond pattern hands are very early examples, but it is perfectly possible that they are replacements. Diamond pattern brass or steel hands seem to have been the most popular type of replacement hands fitted. The writer has often found hands of this type fitted to both bracket and longcase clocks of earlier periods. The dial of the Ellicott clock is of engraved and polished brass fitted with enamel subsidiary dials. The dial of Pykes' clock is of engraved and silvered brass. It will be seen that there is a central date hand, a not uncommon feature on clocks with silvered dials. Pyke's clock probably dates *circa* 1775.

Thomas Chantler is a maker about whom little is known. Plates IV/55, IV/56 and IV/57 illustrate a quarter striking clock which is unusual in two respects. It is fitted with a form of tic-tac escapement. The tic-tac escapement works well enough but long term was not as satisfactory as the verge or anchor. It was used at the end of the seventeenth century by Knibb, Tompion and one or two other well-known makers, but none of them persisted with it. Chantler's version is slightly different in construction to the early examples. The second unusual feature of Chantler's clock is that it shows seconds in the arch. The seconds hand is a replacement.

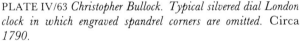

PLATE IV/63 *Christopher Bullock. Typical silvered dial London clock in which engraved spandrel corners are omitted.* Circa *1790.*

PLATE IV/64 *William Smith. Large ebonised musical clock whose French style door surround and plain silvered dial plate make an unusual contrast with the conventional bell-top case.* Circa *1790.*

Plate IV/58 shows another, more conventional, clock by Thomas Chantler. A feature to note in this clock is that the spandrels fitted to the brass dial plate give the impression that they are part of the dial plate. In fact they are separate castings screwed to the dial plate, but some later eighteenth century dial plates of this type are made all in one piece with spandrels which form an integral part of the dial plate which fits over the enamel dials. Compare this dial with that shown in in Plate IV/71, which is of the type just described. Thomas Chantler is not listed by Baillie or Loomes but his entry in Britten reads:

'Chantler — London; about 1750. Hatton speaks with admiration of his watches.'

There are several Hattons listed in the eighteenth century. Both the Thomas Chantler clocks described appear to have been made near the end of the eighteenth century.

Yet another variation in dial design is shown in Plate IV/59. This is a handsome conventional mahogany clock made *circa* 1795 by the brothers Melly and Martin. It has exceptionally fine gilded brass mounts and fine sound frets. The style of the minutes and the hands indicates a date *circa* 1795. But instead of a chapter ring there is an applied chapter plate. The silvering solution

PLATE IV/65 *Ranger. Sweep centre seconds. Dead-beat escapement. Musical movement playing choice of eight tunes changing automatically every two hours. Curtain in arch rises to reveal automata of two fiddlers and Harlequin and Columbine.* Circa *1795.*

normally used in those days gave a very white appearance. When it was first made the dial of this clock could easily have been taken for a clock with enamel dials. Plate IV/61 shows a clock with a silvered and engraved brass dial made *circa* 1790 which could easily be taken for an enamel dial or indeed for a painted dial. The dotted minutes and design of the hands suggest a date *circa* 1790 for this clock but the makers, Haley and Son, are listed as working before 1774 by Baillie, whereas Britten records Haley and Son in Wigmore Street, London, in 1832. The date suggested by the writer is supported by the fact that the clock has verge escapement and a backplate engraved with scrolling leaves around a basket of fruit. In 1832 this case style and hands would have been most unusual, the backplate would almost certainly have been plain and the clock would have been fitted with an anchor escapement.

The graceful design of the door surround of the large (30 inches high) ebonised clock by William Smith, Plate IV/64, is used to complement the dial design and forms an effective contrast with the vertical lines of the case. This is a musical clock. The tune selector is in the arch. The twin subsidiaries are for chime/not chime and strike/silent. The movement has eight pillars and plays one of the seven tunes every hour, or at will via a pinned cylinder operating twenty-three hammers sounding on twelve bells. The escapement is verge. The backplate is engraved with leafy scrolls, flowerheads and strapwork. There were, inevitably, several William Smiths working at the end of the eighteenth century. This example was probably made *circa* 1790.

William Smith's clock is undoubtedly complicated and complex but it pales into insignificance when compared with the 26 inches high ebonised bracket clock by Ranger, London, shown in Plate IV/65. The painted dial plate of this three train clock is mounted with a 7 inch enamel dial which shows the hours and minutes at the bottom of the dial. The sweep centre hand shows seconds and half seconds around the circumference of the dial. The reason for the half seconds indication is that the dead-beat escapement beats half seconds. The reason for the dead-beat escapement is that a recoil escapement would give a magnified backward movement at each beat to the long sweep centre hand.[12] The enamel dial also shows which of the eight tunes available is being played, days of the month and chime/not chime. All the hands are gilt. The tune played changes automatically every two hours. But this is not all. The full arch has a curtain which slowly rises to reveal the automaton figures of two fiddlers and Harlequin and Columbine at the start of each tune. The curtain falls at the end of the performance. The pin drum of the movement, set at right angles to the plates, operates twelve bells and hammers. The backplate and cocks are engraved with leafy scrolls and flowers. The case is decorated with fine gilded brass mounts. It is similar to the cases shown in Plates IV/53 and IV/54. Michael Ranger is listed in Marylebone, London, 1774-1820. This clock dates *circa* 1795.

Break-arch Clocks 1775-1800

Break-arch cases came into their own during the period now under review.

The first clock in this sequence, Plate IV/66, is a good quality typical break-arch clock made *circa* 1770 by Burtt Wade of London. The case is ebonised fruitwood. The hands, matted dial centre, rococo spandrels and maker's name plaque are exactly what you might expect at this date. The movement has the usual verge escapement. The backplate is engraved with a Chinaman sitting under a parasol, mythical birds, a bridge and two pagodas, all amid leafy scrolls and flowers. The maker's name is signed on the backplate in a reserve.

12. There is another type of escapement, the French *coup perdu*, which allows a half second beating pendulum to indicate seconds on the dial. Although effective, it does not seem to have been used very often in English bracket clocks.

129

Additionally the engraver has signed: 'Boyce sculpt'. This clock is only 13½ inches high.

Thomas Monkhouse was the maker of the mahogany musical clock shown in Plate IV/67. It was probably made between 1770 and 1775. The canted and reeded corners with brass stopping are a feature sometimes found on both longcase and bracket clocks at this time. The feet are of a type usually found on Regency bracket clocks. They and the acorn finials are probably later replacements, though finials are not unknown on eighteenth century break-arch cases. The top of the case is embellished with three moulded panels. Pad tops, as these are called, are another feature sometimes found on break-arch cases. Sometimes the pads are brass bound. These pads, though often there is only one, are frequently made to be removeable, being held in place by a wooden turnbuckle which could be rotated to free the pad. It is fairly uncommon to find a break-arch case housing a three train movement. This example plays a choice of six airs on ten bells and is also fitted with rise and fall regulation. The clock stands 18½ inches high. The backplate is signed: 'Thos. Monkhouse, real nephew and succr' to the late Mr. J. Monkhouse.'

PLATE IV/66 *Burtt Wade. Typical small break-arch clock in ebonised case made* circa *1770.*

PLATE IV/67 *Thomas Monkhouse. Musical movements are not usually housed in normal size pad top break-arch cases. This example is an exception. Feet and finials probably later replacements.* Circa *1775.*

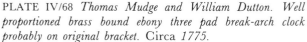

PLATE IV/68 *Thomas Mudge and William Dutton. Well proportioned brass bound ebony three pad break-arch clock probably on original bracket. Circa 1775.*

PLATE IV/69 *William Berridge. Plain unengraved dial centre. Small quarter chiming clocks in break-arch cases are fairly rare. 16in. (40.6cm) high. Circa 1780.*

Plate IV/68 illustrates an ebony three pad brass bound break-arch clock standing on what is probably its original bracket. The makers are Thomas Mudge and William Dutton, who were in partnership *circa* 1755-90. Both were famous makers. The writer dates this clock *circa* 1775. This clock was in the Wetherfield Collection. Britten dated it about 1780 but Bruton, in *The Wetherfield Collection of Clocks*, suggested *circa* 1770. The overall height of the clock, including the bracket, is 21 inches. This is a small and well-proportioned clock.

The clock shown in Plate IV/69 by William Berridge is another example of one of the fairly rare quarter striking break-arch clocks. It is small, 16 inches high, and chimes the quarters on eight bells. The unengraved dial centre, hands and spandrels suggest a date of *circa* 1780. The clock is shown before the Cuthbert clock in Plate IV/70 as a reminder that during this period there is

PLATE IV/70 *John Cuthbert. Traditional dial with rare day of week feature. Dark honey-coloured fruitwood three pad break-arch case.* Circa *1785.*

PLATE IV/71 *Weeks. Quarter chiming clock with sweep centre seconds and adjustable half second dead-beat escapement. The spandrels are cast as an integral part of the gilded dial plate.* Circa *1790.*

much overlapping of styles. John Cuthbert's clock can be dated *circa* 1785 as Cuthbert is thought to have started working in 1784. The clock movement bears a repair date of 1790. The day of the week dial is an unusual and attractive feature which is neatly balanced by the date dial above the hands. This clock is small, just 13½ inches high. The case is of fruitwood of a rich dark honey colour.

Many of the honey-toned fruitwood bracket clocks of the 1760-1800 period are fruitwood clocks that were formerly ebonised, i.e. black clocks that have now faded to an often attractive brown colour. But a number of fruitwood veneered clocks made between about 1780 and 1800 show no signs inside or outside their cases to suggest they were once ebonised. It is thought that these are fruitwood veneered clocks that were originally stained and polished to a rich brown tone using a special varnish finish.

Colour Plate 18 shows a typical good quality mahogany break-arch clock, 15 inches high, signed 'Vulliamy, London 503'. It was probably made by Benjamin Vulliamy *circa* 1785. This is a quarter striking clock chiming on six bells. It is fitted with an adjustable form of half dead-beat escapement introduced by Vulliamy[13] towards the end of the eighteenth century. This is a variation of the dead-beat escapement invented by Graham *circa* 1730. The enamel dial and subsidiary dials are mounted on an engraved brass plate fitted with traditional cast brass corner spandrels.

13. There is a fuller description in *The Country Life International Dictionary of Clocks*, Alan Smith.

PLATE IV/72 *Thomas Wagstaffe. Miniature clocks are a rarity. This example is musical too. Height 7½ in (19.1cm). Enamel dial, burr-elm case.* Circa 1780.

PLATE IV/73 *Rear view of Thomas Wagstaffe's miniature clock.*

The dial of the brass mounted ebonised break-arch clock, by Weeks, London, Plate IV/71, differs from the Vulliamy clock apart from the additional calendar dial. The gilded dial plate is here cast in one piece to include the raised decoration usually represented, as was the case on the Vulliamy clock, by detachable spandrels. The spandrel corner raised decorations here used are an attractively formed chain of husks and baskets reminiscent of the pastoral brass dial surrounds of French longcase clocks of the nineteenth century.[14] The difference of course is that the French brass dial surrounds are made of fragile thin pressed-out brass. The clock is fitted with a half second dead-beat escapement which is adjustable and mounted on the backplate. It is evident that Weeks too was experimenting with the dead-beat escapement. Some form of dead-beat escapement, as explained earlier when discussing the clock by Ranger, Plate IV/65, is necessary on any clock fitted with a sweep centre seconds hand but the usual reason for fitting a dead-beat escapement such as that on the Vulliamy clock was that the dead-beat gave better timekeeping than the anchor, which in turn was more accurate than the verge. At the time these clocks were made a well-to-do household would have contained several clocks, which meant that the advantages of the verge, its tolerance of being moved and of uneven levels, were largely negated.

The verge still persisted in bracket clocks until the end of the eighteenth century, probably through habit and conservatism, but the interest of makers

14. La Comtoise, La Morbier, La Morez, F. Maitzner and J. Moreau.

COLOUR PLATE 16 *Thomas Hunter. An excellent example of a probably Birmingham-made decorated painted dial. Mahogany case.* Circa *1790.*

such as Vulliamy in bracket clocks with more accurate timekeeping is a pointer to the anchor escapement which would shortly, *circa* 1800, begin to replace the verge. The dead-beat escapement needs to be very well made and carefully set-up. It is also more easily damaged than the anchor. For these reasons the anchor, long the mainstay of longcase clocks, eventually triumphed over both verge and dead-beat in bracket clocks.

There are several makers called Weeks. This clock was probably made by the John Weeks listed 1790-94 in St. Swithin's Lane, London. The clock is quarter chiming on eight bells and stands 17 inches high. It dates *circa* 1790. One last point of interest — it will be noted that Weeks' clock is effectively a transitional clock between the break-arch and the arch-top design. The breaks in the arch and indeed the dial are only just perceptible.

Plates IV/72 and IV/73 show a miniature musical clock only 7½ inches high made *circa* 1780 by Thomas Wagstaffe, London. One of four tunes is available every three hours. The attractive burr elm case has a three pad top and fine brass mounts. The dial is of enamel. There is no official size at which a clock

COLOUR PLATE 17 *Daniel De Saint Leu. Backplate and musical work of the clock shown in Plate IV/31.*

is defined as miniature but generally speaking any clock less than 9 inches high could qualify. The clock in Plate IV/74, an ebonised example, has an enamel dial set on a brass dial plate. The clock is 10½ inches high and can thus be classed only as very small. The case style is unusual. This is an ordinary striking clock made *circa* 1785, originally with a verge escapement, by Thomas Best of Lewes in Sussex. Thomas Best's name was no doubt originally painted on the enamel dial but now survives only on the scroll engraved backplate. Bracket clocks are usually signed on either the dial or the backplate or on both. Clocks that were signed only on their painted or enamel dials have frequently lost their names, though sometimes they can be found written on the back of the dial as an instruction to the dial painter. Bracket clocks which started life with no maker's name anywhere are extremely unusual.

Thomas Wright in the Poultry, London, was Free of the Clockmakers' Company in 1770 and died while on a visit to Birmingham in 1792, though his name continued to appear in trade directories until 1794. He was a Quaker. The clock in Plate IV/75 has a convex enamel dial revealed by opening the door that covers the front of the mahogany case. The Sheraton-style inlay is an attractive feature. The style of the hands suggests a date *circa* 1790. Plate IV/76 shows another clock, the maker's name rubbed from the dial, of the same period with Sheraton-style inlays, but clocks with cases of this type, which began to appear *circa* 1790, usually have brass frets below the dial. Slightly earlier versions may have a plain door like that of the example by William Bull of Stratford illustrated by Cescinsky and Webster. Plates IV/77, IV/78 and IV/79 show a small, 13 inches high, ebonised clock by Thomas Church of Norwich made *circa* 1790. The dial in this instance is of convex engraved and silvered brass.

Plate IV/80 shows that even *circa* 1795 there was still a demand for the traditional clock with chapter ring, spandrels and a matted dial centre. But the dotted minutes, the hand design and late but very effective style of engraving (Plate IV/81) plus, of course, the later design of the feet, leave us in no doubt that this fine mahogany three pad clock was made towards the end of the century. Francis Robotham is noted working in Hampstead from *circa* 1790 until 1824.

Plates IV/82, IV/84, IV/85 and IV/86 show three provincial engraved and silvered dial mahogany break-arch bracket clocks, plus a fourth in an ebonised case, made probably between 1790 and 1800. All of them have many points of similarity, yet none are exactly alike. We may be reasonably sure, however, that hands, bracket feet, handles, fish-scale side frets and other case fittings could be obtained if required from wholesale suppliers. Equally it is highly likely, as was suggested in Chapter I, that books of patterns were widely available for the various trades so that a clockmaker could choose the latest hand design, an engraver the latest dial and backplate engraving and the case maker the current case designs and fitments. These might be modified in manufacture but at least they would look up to date. None of these makers, Greenwood of Rochester, John Thackwell of Cardiff, Charles Bayles of Margate or Harris of Chippenham appear among the makers' names listed by

PLATE IV/74 *Thomas Best. Lewes. Very small unusually shaped case 10in. (25.4cm) high. The name has been rubbed off the enamel dial. Circa 1785.*

PLATE IV/75 *(below) Wright. Mahogany break-arch Sheraton-style case that is a development of the case style attributed to Ellicott. (Example Plate II/49.) Case door opens to reveal circular enamel dial. Circa 1790.*

PLATE IV/76 *(below right) Another Sheraton-style case. The feet are of a type that began to appear towards the end of the eighteenth century. Circa 1795.*

COLOUR PLATE 18 *Vulliamy. Small mahogany break-arch clock. Quarter chimes on six bells. Adjustable half dead-beat type of escapement. Enamel dials on brass dial plate.* Circa *1785.*

COLOUR PLATE 19 *(right) Richard Webster. Balloon clock. Satinwood case with inlaid flower head. Fine brass mounts. Enamel dial.* Circa *1795.*

138

PLATE IV/77 *Thomas Church. Norwich. Small ebonised break-arch clock with convex silvered brass dial. Circa 1790.*

PLATE IV/78 *(below right) The backplate of the Thomas Church clock. The basket of plenty is a recurrent popular theme.*

PLATE IV/79 *The movement of the Thomas Church clock.*

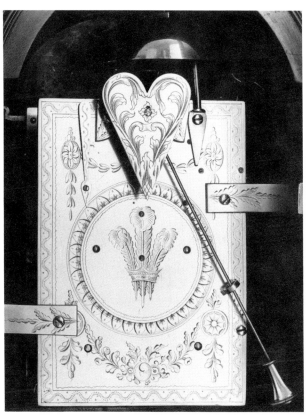

PLATE IV/80 *Francis Robotham. Hampstead. Late example of a traditional dial. Good three pad mahogany break-arch case. Circa 1795.*

PLATE IV/81 *Very attractively engraved backcock apron and backplate of the Francis Robotham clock. Pull-repeat lever just visible top left of photograph.*

Buggins and Turner as having been supplied by Thwaites, though it is possible that some movements were provided by other London wholesalers whose records no longer exist. But certainly the suggestions outlined would account, for example, for the similarities as well as the differences between Greenwood's backplate, Plate IV/83 and that by Robotham in Plate IV/81.

Plate IV/87 shows a mahogany clock by Benjamin Dunkley of Tooting, made *circa* 1790, that looks like a painted dial clock. In fact it has an engraved and silvered brass dial but features Arabic hour numerals which can occur from this period onwards. The engraved spandrel corners are quite clearly based on contemporary painted dial corners. Tooting must have been just a little village four or five miles from the City in those days. Benjamin Dunkley is known to have made a musical longcase.

Five more clocks, by Baker, London in a mahogany case, Plate IV/88; by Richard Ward of Winchester also in mahogany, Plate IV/89; by Thomas Field of Bath in an ebonised case, Plate IV/90; Charles Sheerer of London in a fruitwood case, Plate IV/91; and Allam of London in an ebonised case, Plate IV/92, betray many similarities, though it should be noted that Charles Sheerer's clock retains a normal chapter ring rather than the applied chapter plate borne by two of the other clocks. Allam of London's clock has further

PLATE IV/82 *John Greenwood. Rochester. Provincial mahogany break-arch pad top clock. Silvered engraved dial. Between 1790 and 1800.*

PLATE IV/83 *Backplate of John Greenwood's clock. Engraving typical of period.*

PLATE IV/84 *John Thackwell. Cardiff. Ebonised break-arch pad top case. Silvered engraved dial. Backplate (not shown) engraved with scrolls and a Masonic symbol. Masonic devices are sometimes found on dials or backplates. Between 1790 and 1800.*

PLATE IV/85 *Charles Bayles. Margate. Mahogany pad top break-arch case. Silvered engraved dial. Between 1790 and 1800.*

PLATE IV/86 *Harris. Chippenham. A fourth provincial clock with a silvered engraved dial. Between 1790 and 1800. Many similarities between these last four clocks but none exactly alike.*

PLATE IV/87 *Benjamin Dunkley. Tooting. Mahogany break-arch case. Silvered dial engraved entirely in manner of contemporary decorated painted dial. Arabic numerals. Circa 1790.*

PLATE IV/88 *Baker. Late example of traditional dial with chapter plate and spandrels. Mahogany break-arch case. Between 1790 and 1800.*

PLATE IV/89 *Richard Ward. Winchester. Late provincial example of traditional dial with chapter plate and spandrels. Break-arch mahogany case. Hatched minutes. Fine gilt hands. Between 1790 and 1800.*

PLATE IV/90 *Thomas Field. Bath. Another traditional dial. Hands, if original, suggest date* circa *1785. Ebonised pad top break-arch case.*

PLATE IV/91 *Charles Sheerer. Traditional chapter ring and spandrels. Central date hand. Plain silvered dial centre. Fruitwood pad top break-arch case. Between 1790 and 1800.*

PLATE IV/92 *Allam. Plainer engraved silvered dial. Delicate hands. Quarter chiming clock in pad top ebonised break-arch case. Good brass mounts. Between 1790 and 1800.*

PLATE IV/93 *Thomas de la Salle. Full arch traditional dial indicating that clock runs for fifteen days. Shaped surmount and canted reeded corners of mahogany break-arch case. Between 1790 and 1800.*

PLATE IV/94 *John Taylor. Silvered engraved full arch dial. Musical movement. Case similar to Plate IV/93. Between 1790 and 1800.*

differences in dial design. Thomas Field of Bath, alone among these five makers, is known to have ordered a few clocks from Thwaites of London, though it is not known whether this clock is one of them. Richard Ward of Winchester's clock has hatched minutes and notable and unusual gilt hands. Again, although there are many superficial similarities, there are many differences of detail. These five clocks were probably all made betwen 1790 and 1800, save for that by Thomas Field of Bath whose hands suggest it may have been made a few years earlier. Thomas Field started working in 1773 and continued until 1812.

Plate IV/93 shows an unusual full arch dial mahogany clock with a shaped surmount in place of a pad top and handles fitted to the sides of the case. The maker is Thomas de la Salle of London who was working from 1780 until 1818. The canted and reeded brass stopped corners of this case may seem by now, *circa* 1790, a rather old fashioned feature on bracket clocks but they continued to occur. De la Salle was clearly an individualist, his dial shows a day calendar marked with the suggestion that the clock should be wound in the middle and at the end of the month. Nearly all Georgian bracket clocks are of eight day duration but this example runs for fifteen days between windings. Long duration, i.e. month or longer going, bracket clocks are very seldom seen, though Tompion made a year-going bracket clock. Plate IV/94 shows a fairly

PLATE IV/95 *Leroux. Well-known maker of balloon clocks. Later example of early type balloon case with break-sided outline to case. Anchor escapement. Fine winged claw feet. Enamel dial.* Circa *1790.*

PLATE IV/96 *Barwise. Example of second-type of balloon case with no break-sided effect. Quarter chiming. Satinwood banded with kingwood case.* Circa *1790.*

similar clock but here the full arch of the dial is used for the chime/not chime and tune selection levers. Evidently this is a musical clock. The maker is John Taylor, London. Once again the dial is of engraved and silvered brass.

Balloon Clocks

It is not known when the first balloon clocks made their appearance, though conjecturally it was some years after the Marot inspired French-style clock made *circa* 1765 by Justin Vulliamy that is illustrated in Plate IV/10. What is more certain, to judge from surviving examples, is that balloon cased clocks enjoyed their greatest vogue between about 1780 and 1810. This is not to suggest that balloon clocks ever became particularly popular, they did not, but this was almost certainly due to the difficulty and expense of making a case with so many curved veneered surfaces rather than to the design itself which is particularly graceful and elegant.

Balloon clocks fall into two categories. The first to appear were those in which the circular section containing the dial and movement appear to sit upon the base. There is a definite break in the line between the two main constituent parts. A typical example of this type of balloon case is shown in Plate IV/95.

It was made by John Leroux, who made many balloon clocks, most of which were in ebonised cases which were less expensive to produce. Leroux is thought to have been working by 1750 but was a member of the Clockmakers' Company from 1781 until 1808. The clock illustrated has good brass mounts and an enamel dial. As is usually the case with balloon clocks, it is fitted with an anchor escapement. The narrower swing of an anchor controlled pendulum is obviously better suited to a waisted case than the wide swing of the verge bob pendulum. This clock was probably made between 1785 and 1800, though the writer has seen earlier examples by this maker in similar cases. The break-arch sided type of balloon case, still, as suggested earlier in the chapter, betraying the early eighteenth century French origin of the style, was joined *circa* 1785 by the now completely Anglicized second type of case in which the drum-shaped top of the clock joins the base in an uninterrupted sweep. The clock by Barwise, Plate IV/96, is a good example. Obviously there are minor variations of each of these two main styles. Both types of case continued to be made during the rest of the Georgian period.

Colour Plate 19 shows a much grander balloon clock of the second type. It stands 24 inches high and is veneered in satinwood with crossbanded borders. The waist is inlaid with a fine stylised flower head. The brass bezels, handles and trellis fret of the painted concave superstructure make a good contrast with the mellow colour of the case. This clock too has an anchor escapement. It is signed on the backplate 'Richard Webster, Exchange Alley, London'. The enamel dial, to avoid clutter, is signed simply 'Webster, London'. Richard Webster, a member of a famous clockmaking family, was Free in 1779 and worked until 1807.

The clock by Barwise, illustrated in Plate IV/96, and the unsigned example in Plate IV/97 also have satinwood cases. They and the Webster clock just described were made between 1785 and 1800. The first satinwood period of English furniture was between about 1780 and 1810. These three clocks have another characteristic in common. They have a pronounced Sheraton look to them. They are visibly in tune with contemporary cabinet making and there can be no doubt that in expensive examples such as these the case took precedence over the clock. Even so, a fine case would be fitted with a high quality clock movement. Indeed the Barwise clock quarter chimes on eight bells.

Plate IV/98, a balloon clock by John Baker of Covent Garden, London, illustrates another break-sided case with typical Sheraton style inlays but the case in this instance is of mahogany.

Two Precision Bracket Clocks

The great majority of bracket clocks were made for domestic use. It has been the writer's intention throughout this study to concentrate on such clocks. Those interested in clocks outside the mainstream of normal production, or particularly interested in unusual escapements, can start to widen their knowledge by visiting the British Museum, where there is an excellent

PLATE IV/97 *Unsigned. Another fine satinwood case with inlaid flower head. Good brass mounts.* Circa *1795*.

PLATE IV/98 *John Baker. A later example of the earlier type of balloon case. Mahogany with shell inlay.* Circa *1790*.

collection of clocks, and by joining the Antiquarian Horological Society. The two examples now briefly described can both be seen at the British Museum.

Plates IV/99, IV/100 and IV/101 illustrate a timepiece ebonised mahogany bracket clock made by Josiah Emery. Emery was a noted maker of Swiss origin. He was born *circa* 1725 and died in 1797. This clock was made *circa* 1780 and stands 17½ inches high. The front panel of the case is hinged. At first sight this is a conventional bracket clock, though it will be noted that the dial indicates seconds. It is when the movement is examined that the considerable differences between this and the conventional bracket clocks of the period are seen. The pendulum is large and very heavy and is fitted with a type of zinc and steel temperature compensation. The movement is exquisitely made and finished. Friction is reduced to a minimum and the escapement pivots are jewelled. Harrison's maintaining power is fitted. The escapement is the French *coup perdu*[15] type, which allows seconds to be shown from a half second beating

15. This clock is described in greater detail and the action of the *coup perdu* escapement illustrated and lucidly explained in *A Precision Clock* by Josiah Emery. By J.L. Evans, by courtesy of the Trustees of the British Museum. *Antiquarian Horology.* Summer 1980.

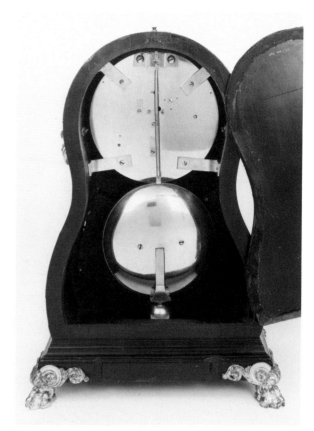

PLATE IV/100 *Backplate and zinc/steel compensated pendulum of Emery's clock.*

PLATE IV/99 *(left) Josiah Emery. Precision timepiece ebonised mahogany bracket clock with seconds dial. Front panel hinged to allow easy access to pendulum.* Circa *1780.*

pendulum. It is constructed in such a way that great accuracy is obtained. Although this clock stands on a bracket high precision bracket clocks of this ilk are usually referred to as table regulators.

Plates IV/102 and IV/103 illustrate a timepiece ebonised break-arch bracket clock, made *circa* 1765, by Thomas Mudge. Thomas Mudge was the inventor, *circa* 1759, of the lever escapement used in countless succeeding generations of watches. Mudge was born in Exeter in 1715, the son of a clergyman schoolmaster. It was soon realised that he showed considerable mechanical ability. Accordingly he was apprenticed to George Graham, Tompion's successor. In later years Mudge left most of the running of his business to William Dutton, another ex-Graham apprentice with whom he had formed a partnership. He moved to Plymouth in 1771 where he concentrated on marine timekeepers. He died in 1794.

PLATE IV/101 *Movement of Emery's clock showing* coup perdu *escapement.*

The main interest in Mudge's ebonised bracket clock[16] (Plates IV/102 and IV/103) lies in the lever escapement, an early example, and the lunar work. The escapement of the clock is driven by a *remontoire*, a subsidiary spring which is rewound by the mainspring every seven and a half minutes. A *remontoire* ensures that the power delivered to the escapement remains as constant as possible. Temperature compensation is fitted; a pair of brass and steel laminated strips act on one of the two balance springs. The dial shows seconds, the month of the year and the lunar day. The lunar dial has a tidal indicator and shows

16. Described in greater detail in *Some Outstanding Clocks over 700 Years*, H. Alan Lloyd. Leonard Hill. 1958. Catalogued and described in *Five Centuries of British Timekeeping*. Goldsmiths Hall, London. October 1955.

PLATE IV/102 *Thomas Mudge's famous, probably unique, lever escapement timepiece bracket clock with* remontoire, *temperature compensation and lunar and tidal work. Once the property of Isambard Kingdom Brunel.* Circa *1765.*

the age and phase of the moon to an accuracy of one fifth of a second in twenty nine and a half days. Mudge wished to provide an extremely accurate lunar indication because of the application of this indication to navigation.

The case of this clock is easily removed. There are three inspection panels in the top of the case. This possibly unique and celebrated timepiece was once owned by Isambard Kingdom Brunel.

PLATE IV/103 *A view of the movement of the Thomas Mudge clock.*

CHAPTER FIVE

The Export Trade

The export trade in English clocks was established before the end of the seventeenth century. Tompion went to Holland, presumably on business, in 1697. It is recorded[1] that the Royal Family ordered clocks and watches by him as presents for dignitaries in Algiers, Tripoli and Tunis and for the Duke of Florence, Cosimo III, Grand Duke of Tuscany and last but one of the Medicis. Early in the eighteenth century George, Prince of Denmark, became a client. Clocks by Tompion have been found in Holland, France, Spain, Italy and Russia. No doubt more are still waiting to be discovered in other countries.

The early export trade was by no means limited to Tompion. Many other leading London makers sold clocks and watches into Europe. The writer's wife discovered a longcase clock made *circa* 1685 by John Ebsworth in the vestry of the church of Santo Stefano in Venice. Several clocks by Christopher Gould and other late seventeenth century London makers are known with dials inscribed in Italian or Spanish. Indeed, a few early English clockmakers even established themselves abroad.[2] Ignatius Huggeford was working in Florence by 1686. A lantern clock by him is inscribed: 'Ign. Huggeford nella Galleria del Gran Duca di Toscana Englesse'. Another is signed: 'Ignatius Huggeford Florentia fecit'. By 1675 Joseph Norris was working in Amsterdam where he made longcase, bracket and Hague clocks as well as at least one lantern clock inscribed 'Joseph Norris Amsterdam'. Robert Hynam went to Russia some time before 1776 where he became clockmaker to the Royal Court. The gifted but unlucky Henry Sully, who had been apprenticed to Charles Gretton, was commissioned to direct a factory at Versailles in 1718. He arranged for sixty London watch and clockmakers and their families to go to France with him. Sully was not a success. He and his staff of workmen returned to England two years later. Sully was a brilliant clockmaker but was not a good businessman. He died in 1728.

Nor was the trade limited to Europe. Dawson[3] described and illustrated a thirty hour timepiece alarum by Christopher Gould with Turkish numerals made *circa* 1685.

Possibly the first attempt to export a clock to Turkey was made by Sir John Finch, a British ambassador to Turkey, who offered the gift of an English clock to the Grand Vizier in 1680. The Grand Vizier was expecting the gift of a large sum of money. The clock was refused.[4]

Turkish market bracket clocks, i.e. those with Turkish numerals on their dials intended for the Near East, the Turkish Empire and Persia, eventually

1 *Thomas Tompion. His Life and Work*, R.W. Symonds.
2 *English Lantern Clocks*, George White. Antique Collectors' Club, 1989.
3 'Repatriated English Clocks', P.G. Dawson. *Antiquarian Horology*, September 1982.
4 'Under the Turk in Constantinople. A record of Sir. John Finch's Embassy 1674-1681', G.F. Abbott. (Noted by O. Kurz.)

accounted for a considerable portion of the business of a number of London makers. Dawson noted George and Edward Prior, Francis Perigal, Markwick Markham, Paul Rimbault, Recordon and Spencer and Perkins. Kurz[5] lists Benjamin Barber, Henton Brown, Robert Best, Henry Borrell, George Clarke, Robert Markham, Richard Peckover, Markwick Markham-Perigal, Francis Perigal, George Prior, Recordon, Isaac Rogers, Daniel Torin and Vulliamy. These were makers exporting musical clocks and, it can be presumed, non-musical bracket clocks. There was a considerable trade too in watches and longcases.

It is interesting to note that Kurz cites Eric Bruton[6] '...There is considerable similarity among the movements of musical clocks of the later eighteenth century for the Turkish Market and it seems reasonably certain that they were all made by the same supplier, Thwaites and Reed of Clerkenwell, despite different makers names on the dials.' Kurz continues '...This is amply confirmed by the Day books of this still existing firm which are now in the Guildhall Library'. (MS. 6788) These day books start in 1780 and show that Thwaites and Reed did indeed supply 'the trade' with musical clocks for the Turkish market, not just the movements or barrels but the complete clocks in their decorated cases ready for dispatch. Most of the famous clockmakers of the time appear among their customers.

Some of the examples of Thwaites and Reed orders cited from the Day books by Kurz give an interesting insight into the terminology of the day: '...The firm of Spencer and Perkins paid on August 2, 1782 for "Three eight Day Clocks with White Diall Plates engraved in Turky Characters and Engraved at the corners.." Mr. Recordon paid Febuary 10, 1788 for "Two spring One tune Clocks with Japann'd Plates." (painted dials) "..The two cases...Japann'd for the Turky Trade and with Festoon corners." Mr. Isaac Rogers on March 14,1789, for "A new Spring Six Tune Chime clock... Centre enamell for the Hours with Turky Characters." '

Clocks with automata and large organ clocks with highly complicated automata were also made. It seems likely that some of this work was sub-contracted out to smaller specialist workshops. No doubt there were also other trade makers and suppliers of musical and complicated clocks in spite of Bruton's comments.

It is generally considered that the most important name in the 'Turkey' trade was George Prior. The writer and his wife once dined with a distinguished elderly Turkish couple on the island of Heybeliada in the sea of Marmara. Their host spoke of the 'Georgy Priorys' he owned. They were produced for inspection. They were pocket watches by different makers. Realisation dawned. A 'Georgy Priory' was a watch just as watches were sometimes called 'Tompions' in the early eighteenth century.

Many bracket clocks exported to the Near East have made their way back to England. Some have been brought back by travellers but Dawson in his article 'Repatriated English Clocks', explained that J.C. Hirst, an English businessman who made frequent visits to Turkey in the 1920s, arranged to purchase English export trade clocks that were brought to his attention. By

5 *European Clocks and Watches in the Near East*, O. Kurz. The Warburg Institute. University of London. 1975. E.J. Brill. Leiden.
6 *Clocks and Watches 1400-1900*, Eric Bruton, 1967.

PLATE V/1 *Pedro Higgs y Diego Evans. Junto Ala. Bolsa Real. Londres. (Peter Higgs and David Evans. Sweeting's Alley. Royal Exchange. London). All Spanish inscription on a four train quarter chiming and musical clock for the Spanish market.* Circa *1780.*

PLATE V/2 *Diego Evans (David Evans). Another typical Spanish market quarter chiming clock. Painted dial. Eight bell chime. strike/silent in Spanish.* Circa *1785.*

1929 J.C. Hirst had arranged for his agent, Rifaat Imbrahim, to open a shop in the Grand Bazaar, Istanbul, from whence he was able to report his finds.

The clocks re-imported by Hirst were all sold. They and other Turkish market clocks that have found their way back to Britain have frequently had their Turkish numeral chapter rings re-engraved on the reverse side or replaced with conventional English chapter rings. Colour Plate 21 is an example. Enamel dials were also anglicised. But as we shall see, clocks made for the Near East often have other distinguishing features.

Europe and the Near East were not the only market to be developed by English clockmakers. There was also a lively trade in clocks for China and other oriental countries which will be described later in this chapter. Clocks

COLOUR PLATE 20 *Daniel Quare. No 32. Double basket top clock with red lacquer case decorated with gilt. Probably for the Italian market. Circa 1715.*

COLOUR PLATE 21 *Francis Perigal. Typical Turkish market red lacquer clock. Crescent finials. Human figures not depicted in lacquer work. Anglicised chapter ring. Circa 1775.*

made for the Near East and China were specifically designed to meet the tastes of their purchasers and often, though not invariably, look quite different to the traditional home-trade English clocks. They are also quite different to each other. But clocks made in London for the European market pander much less to the national tastes of their recipients. The clock by Clark and Dunster, Plate II/25, has its strike/silent ring inscribed in Dutch, as does the Stephen Rimbault clock in Plate II/41. The musical four train clock by Stephen Rimbault in Plate II/44 is inscribed in French, as is Claudius Du Chesne's clock in Plate II/11. These clocks are not markedly different from clocks made for the home market, nor for that matter are the Spanish market clocks shown in Plates V/1 and V/2, though it will be noted that Peter Higgs and David Evans of Sweeting's Alley, Royal Exchange, have become Pedro Higgs y Diego Evans, Junto Ala, Bolsa Real, Londres. Bracket clocks by the Pedro Higgs y Diego Evans partnership appear too in the former South American Spanish colonies but curiously the writer has had no success in tracing any exports of Georgian period English bracket clocks to North America.

Colour Plate 20 illustrates a fine double basket top clock by Daniel Quare made *circa* 1715 and numbered DQ32. The movement has six pillars and repeats on six bells. The backplate is engraved with scrolling leaves around a bird and a mask within formal borders. The case is of red lacquer decorated with gilt. The dial is remarkable for the silvered filigree spandrels. The two lower subsidiary dials indicate the day of the week and the month. None of the subsidiaries are inscribed in Italian but there can be little doubt, to judge from the Italianate appearance of its case, that this clock was made for an Italian client. The clock stands about 20 inches high. Daniel Quare, one of the most illustrious of English makers, was well placed to take export orders. The weddings of his children[7] were attended by the envoys of Venice, Florence, Hanover, Portugal, Sweden, Prussia and Denmark, the Comte de Briancon and the Countess of Guicord. Also present was the Duchess of Marlborough. The Royal Family was only prevented from being present because Quare was a Quaker and they were unable to attend dissenting places of worship. Leaving aside the export connection, it is evident that Quare was held in high esteem socially.

The clock shown in Plate V/3 is intriguing because it was made for the Turkish market by an Englishman, Stephen Thorogood of London, working at Saint Mark's Place, Venice. Stephen Thorogood is also known as Stefano Thorogood, from which it may be presumed he spent some time in Venice. Thorogood, as we know, was not the first English clockmaker in Italy but he was arguably the first to settle in Venice and make a typical bell-top bracket clock for a customer from the Turkish Empire, Near East or Persia. It is surprising that the clock has a typically English-looking mahogany case because Turkish market clocks were usually housed in elaborate cases of tortoiseshell, ebonised pearwood, lacquer, Vernis Martin or even horn or mother-of-pearl. This is one of very few Turkish market examples known to the writer to be housed in a mahogany case. Dawson noted that these clocks were seldom contained in mahogany cases and were never veneered with decorative veneers.

7 *Noted in Chats on Old Clocks*, H. Alan Lloyd. 1951.

PLATE V/3 *Stephen Thorogood. 'At Saint Marks Place. Venice.' Mahogany bell-top bracket clock made for the Turkish market by an expatriate London maker.* Circa *1775.*

PLATE V/4 *Nathaniel Newman. Typical early Turkish market lacquer clock. Human figures avoided in the lacquerwork. Early form of lunar indication.* Circa *1715.*

COLOUR PLATE 22 *George Prior. Rare coral stained horn Turkish market musical clock. Cut glass dome, finials and pillars. Movement stamped 'A.J. Thwaites'. A.J. Thwaites made many musical clocks for the trade. Flower painted dial plate. Enamel dials. Circa 1790.*

COLOUR PLATE 23 *Benjamin Barber. Green Vernis Martin musical clock for the Turkish market. Painted glass cupola top. Circa 1785.*

COLOUR PLATE 24 *George Prior. Cream Vernis Martin musical clock for the Turkish market. Cut glass finials, pillars and cupola. Flower painted dial plate. Enamel dials. Circa 1790.*

COLOUR PLATE 25 *Perigal. Royal Exchange. Red tortoiseshell. Gilt mounted cupola topped clock with automata for the Turkish market. Circa 1795.*

PLATE V/5 *George Clarke. Leadenhall Steet. Rare, small, mother-of-pearl cased clock for the Turkish market.* Circa *1740.*

PLATE V/6 *Edward Pistor. Musical clock. Female figures not shown on the brass corner pieces. Crescent topped pineapple finials. Lacquer case avoids human figures. Turkish market.* Circa *1760.*

Plate V/4 shows an early Turkish market clock made *circa* 1715 by Nathaniel Newman. Apart from the Turkish numerals the clock does not at first sight differ from its home market inverted bell-top lacquer counterparts. Yet, if this case is compared with a typical home market clock such as the inverted bell-top lacquer clock by Abraham Weston of Lewes, Plate III/1, it will be seen that Nathaniel Newman's clock differs in that no human figures appear in the lacquerwork. Equally, the decorative brass corner pieces of Turkish market clocks, Plate V/6 is an example, differ from the usual terms or caryatids in that they too avoid depicting female figures which might have offended local religious sensibilties. The brass finials of Turkish market clocks are often shaped as crescents.

Plate V/5 shows a Turkish market clock made *circa* 1740 by George Clarke of Leadenhall Street. George Clarke was a well-known maker for the Turkish and Eastern markets. This example is of particular interest because it is a miniature clock, 9 inches high, veneered with mother-of-pearl. Mother-of-pearl clocks are extremely rare.

The lacquered bell-top clock by Edward Pistor shown in Plate V/6 is

PLATE V/7 *William Dunant. Equation of time clocks with sweep centre seconds were sometimes made for the Turkish market. This example probably re-imported as the chapter ring has been Anglicised. Ebonised case with male Oriental turbanned head terms. Circa 1765.*

PLATE V/8 *Markwick Markham. Tortoiseshell and gilt mounted musical clock for the Turkish market. Markwick Markham also made clocks for Russia. Circa 1755.*

COLOUR PLATE 26 *John Drury. Four train musical clock with a jack in the cupola top. For the Spanish market.* Circa *1770.*

COLOUR PLATE 27 *Charles Cabrier. A pair of musical and automata clocks in lacquered chinoiserie style waisted cases reputedly made for the King of Nepal.* Circa *1770.*

PLATE V/9 *George Prior. Mahogany cased musical bracket clock with painted dial centre and Oriental turbanned head terms. Mahogany clocks are unusual for the Turkish market.* Circa *1785.*

interesting because it exhibits features from several countries yet is still unmistakably an English musical clock for the Turkish or Near East market. The disparate features are the French style of the dial surround, the Dutch wavy minute band and the crescents fitted to the tops of the pineapple finials. The pineapple was a traditional English symbol of welcome. The brass decorations fitted to the corners of the case do not contain female figures.

Plate V/7 illustrates an equation of time ebonised bell-top bracket clock made for the Turkish market by William Dunant. It dates *circa* 1765 and is

PLATE V/10 *George Clarke.*
Tortoiseshell case, gilt metal
cast volutes. Silk suspended
verge escapement perhaps a
modification. Foliate scroll
engraved backplate. Turkish
market. Circa 1765.

fitted with sweep centre seconds. Clocks with these characteristics were made occasionally for the Turkish market but this example has almost certainly been re-imported and anglicised, as can be seen by the chapter ring. Turkish numerals are retained in the subsidiary dials. Surprisingly, the brass corners are terms, i.e. they depict human heads, but the heads are visibly male, turbanned and Oriental. These Oriental terms are not an isolated example. Plate V/9 shows a mahogany veneered musical clock with a painted dial centre made by George Prior *circa* 1785 fitted with similar terms. They were also sometimes used on home trade clocks.

Plates V/8, 9, 11, 12, 13, 14 and 15 and Colour Plates 22, 23 and 24 illustrate a selection of musical, automata and quarter chiming clocks for the Turkish market. They date between *circa* 1755 and the end of the eighteenth century, at which time the Turkish market started to decline. Several of these clocks exhibit features which merit further description. Colour Plate 22 shows a clock, the case of which is made from coral stained horn. The movement is stamped on the front plate 'A. and J. Thwaites' and both the seven pillar movement and the seatboard are numbered 464. This clock plays one of six tunes at every hour on twelve bells. The backplate is engraved with scrolling leaves around a basket of fruit. The enamel dial plate is mounted on a shaped surround painted with sprays of flowers and is signed 'George Prior London'. The clock stands 31½ inches high and dates *circa* 1790.

Colour Plates 23 and 24 and Plate V/11 show three more musical clocks. The first was made by Benjamin Barber, *circa* 1785. It has a flower painted white dial, a painted glass cupola top and a foliate engraved backplate. It plays one of a choice of four tunes on ten bells. It stands 27½ inches high. The second clock, Colour Plate 24, was made by George Prior *circa* 1790. The white enamel dial and subsidiaries are set on a dial plate painted with flowers. The crystal cupola top is centred by a revolving glass rod. The finials are of crystal. Plate V/11 shows a not dissimilar clock made by the same George Prior, *circa* 1785.

These three clocks all possess dials painted with flowers. Their cases appear at first sight to be lacquered in the usual way but closer examination shows that they too are decorated with flowers and that the general appearance of the lacquer finish is different to the usual English lacquer work. This type of finish is called Vernis Martin.[8] The name derives from four French brothers called Martin, two of whom obtained in 1730 a monopoly for twenty years to produce 'all sorts of relief decoration in the manner of China and Japan'. They perfected a special varnish or lacquer finish, several coats of which were applied, each being rubbed down between applications. Green and red were popular colours but yellow, lilac and other colours were used.

Vernis Martin became a general term describing furniture and other objects painted with flowers and varnished on a varnished ground. Neither oriental motifs nor relief work appear to have been used on clock cases described as Vernis Martin. The work was inspired by the Orient but retains an indisputably French appearance. By 1749 the Martin brothers had been created 'Manufactures Royales' and were commissioned to decorate the Dauphin's Versailles apartments. Eventually they had three workshops in Paris.

Colour Plate 25 and Plate V/13 show two more fine clocks by Perigal and James Cox respectively. Each is housed in a gilt mounted tortoiseshell case. It will be seen that the white enamel dial plates are set against a coloured enamel background. This is a feature which is usually associated with clocks for the Chinese market.

The tortoiseshell clock made by Markwick Markham in partnership with Perigal, shown in Plate V/14, has an enamel dial plate set against a painted background depicting passengers landing from a boat against a background of a minaret. Yet the principal figure has an unmistakably Chinese appearance. Clearly the artist craftsman had become confused. The clock's Turkish purchaser was probably equally confused but perhaps not more so than many of his compatriots whose musical clocks usually played unmistakably English airs.

8 Abridged and paraphrased definition of that given in *The Country Life International Dictionary of Clocks*. Consultant Editor Alan Smith. London, 1979.

PLATE V/11 *George Prior. Elaborate cupola topped Vernis Martin cased musical clock with crescent shaped finials. Painted dial plate. Enamel dials. Turkish market. Circa 1785.*

PLATE V/12 *George Prior. Tortoiseshell cupola topped musical clock probably once with automata. Turkish market. Circa 1790.*

The description 'Turkish market', as already indicated, included the Near East and Persia where a horologist friend of the writer found several English clocks. But clocks were also commissioned from further afield. Colour Plate 27 shows a pair of bracket clocks reputedly made for the King of Nepal. The maker was Charles Cabrier who died in 1777. The clocks were made *circa* 1770. Each has a seven pillar movement playing one of six tunes every hour on twelve bells with twenty-four hammers. The enamel dials are set on dial plates decorated with flowers. The dial arches show automata of craftsmen at work and musical trios. The chinoiserie style waisted cases are surmounted by pierced crestings and flaming urn finials. The cases are lacquered in gilt tones with birds, flowers and trellis work on a brown ground. There are gilt bronze mounts with dragon mask corners and winged paw feet. Each clock stands 30 inches high. A number of clocks were also made for the Indian market and, of course, British officials and traders must have imported clocks for their own use. Clocks that have been in India have usually suffered considerably from the climate and have often been re-cased.

Considerable numbers of English bracket clocks were made for the Chinese market during the eighteenth century but to understand the Chinese trade it is necessary to understand the background.

China was effectively a closed country, completely cut off from the West during the English Georgian period. Three events led to the eventual importation of many fine English clocks. The first of these was that in 1583 a Jesuit priest, Father Matteo Ricci and a companion, Father Ruggieri, were allowed to settle in Chaoh-Ching, to the west of Canton. The Jesuits were intent on bringing Christianity to the Chinese. As part of their campaign to impress the Chinese and gain influence they set up a striking turret clock with a hand visible from the street. The Chinese were totally unacquainted with Western horology and technology. Soon the Jesuits and their 'self ringing bells' became famous.[9] The second event took place in 1601. In that year the Jesuit Fathers arranged to visit the Emperor in order to present him with, among other presents, two clocks, a large iron quarter striking weight driven turret clock and a table clock. Although the Emperor did not deign to meet Ricci and his companions he was already interested in and impressed by the clocks, because he appointed four eunuchs to learn how they were made and how to maintain them. Thereafter the Emperor Wan-Li (1572-1620) took the table clock everywhere with him. He also granted the Jesuits permission to establish a mission in Peking. The weight driven turret clock was installed in a specially built wooden tower.

The interest shown by the Emperor in clocks led, *circa* 1680, during the reign of the Emperor K'ang Hsi (1662-1722), to the establishment of an Imperial watch and clock factory within the palace precincts. The Chinese craftsmen were taught clockmaking by the Jesuits but the Jesuits eventually fell out of favour and in about 1721 they were ordered home, save for those who were scientists or technicians.

The third event was that, in 1600, Queen Elizabeth I granted a charter to a group of merchants to trade with the East Indies. The East India Company

9 By far the best account of the export trade in clocks to China known to the writer is that given by Allen H. Weaving in *Antiquarian Horology*, Summer 1991. His article 'Clocks for the Emperor' was based upon much research and several visits to China. Much of the background information here given is based upon this article and the notes made by the writer during a conversation with Allen Weaving prior to its publication.

169

PLATE V/13 *James Cox and Son. Quarter chiming clock. French style case of tortoise-shell with gilt mounts. Dial decoration more usual for Chinese market clocks. Cox and Son were best known for Chinese market clocks. Turkish market. Circa 1785.*

PLATE V/14 *Markwick Markham and Perigal. Tortoiseshell and gilt mounted clock with painted Oriental scene featuring both a minaret and a Chinese figure. Was the English artist confused? Turkish market. Circa 1790.*

was naturally keen to establish trade with the Far East too, but encountered difficulties in establishing trade with China. It was not until 1715 that a factory was established at Canton. The word factory in this sense was used to describe an office and warehouse belonging to a European merchant, or group of European merchants, in the East rather than a place where goods were manufactured.

The Chinese looked upon China as the centre of the earth. Foreigners were seen as bringing tribute to the Emperor, the son of Heaven. Trade was a privilege and was closely regulated, as were the different levels of influence which ranged from the Chinese merchants at the bottom end of the scale through the merchants' guild or Co-Hoy to the Hoppo, or customs superintendent, to the local governor, then through eight levels of mandarin to the Royal Court. Above the Court was the Emperor. In 1757 trade was confined to Canton by official decree and was limited to three months a year. For the rest of the year the European traders were obliged to live in Macao or return home. The scope for manipulation under these circumstances was considerable. Arrangements had to be made with those local Chinese merchants who were permitted to trade with the Europeans. The Chinese merchants, in their turn, had to make their own arrangements with the many levels of officialdom above them.

It was here that English clocks and watches came into their own. 'Sing Songs' as the 'self ringing bells' were now also known, had royal approval and were much sought after as status symbols. As such they also made excellent tribute and business gifts, though neither the number eventually imported nor those made at the Imperial Factory was ever great enough to establish the European clock or watch as a normal Chinese household artefact during the Georgian era. Nonetheless, as early as 1735 Father Valentin Chalier[10] wrote '.... as for clocks, the Imperial Palace is stuffed with them. Watches, carillons, repeaters, automatic organs, mechanised globes of every conceivable system, — there must be more than four thousand from the best masters of Paris and London, very many of which I have had through my hands for repairs or cleaning.'

Tribute, presents and business gifts, whatever their intrinsic merit, can be difficult items to account for in balance sheets and cargo manifests. The official records of the East India Company give only occasional indications of the shipment of clocks and watches. For example Weaving records that during the 1771 season the East India Company imported seventy clocks into Canton, yet in 1772 the company imported only fourteen clocks. Low levels of pay meant that it was also the normal custom for ships' officers to trade in smaller items. Weaving notes that in 1783 Captain Wordsworth of the *Earl of Sandwich* had clocks and watches in his private cargo for sale in China.

The East India Company was mindful enough of its monopoly to insist that smaller merchants trading into China did not stay from one season to the next. But their presence was no doubt useful to them in many ways, one of which we may be sure was the unrecorded provision of items intended as tribute or business gifts. No doubt many general traders took clocks to China but two

10 Quoted by Allen H. Weaving.

PLATE V/15 *George Prior.*
Tortoiseshell and gilt mounted
musical clock. Flower painted
dial plate. Turkish market.
Circa *1795.*

enterprising London clockmakers, James Cox and his son John Henry,
actually set up a 'factory' in Canton in 1783. They imported complicated
clocks, movements and watches from London and singing bird-cages and
watches from Geneva. They continued to trade in China as James Cox and
Son, Cox and Beale and finally Cox, Beale and Felix Laurent, until 1792.

Changing trade patterns and increasing Chinese manufacture of clocks and
watches meant that by about 1815 the export of British and European clocks
and watches, a trade which Britain had dominated during the eighteenth
century, went into decline.

COLOUR PLATE 28 *W. Staples. Automata clock for the Chinese market. Circa 1790.*

COLOUR PLATE 29 *(right) Unsigned. Quarter chiming and musical clock. Gilt metal case. Dial set with paste jewels. English made for the Chinese market. Circa 1790.*

English Georgian clocks made for the Chinese market are often very complicated with much use of automata. Cases are frequently of gilded metal and heavily decorated. Perhaps because it was feared that enamel dials would be damaged by winding, they are frequently wound from the back. Colour Plate 28 shows a good example, the balance wheel escapement movement is signed 'W. Staples', who is recorded working *circa* 1790. The glass column revolves to give the impression of water. The trees also revolve and there are further automata in the base. There is a sweep centre seconds hand, another feature typically found on Chinese market clocks. It seems that the sweep centre seconds hand was valued by the Chinese because it showed the clock was going. Elaborate clocks actually made in China often have sweep centre hands that make a complete revolution in less or more than a minute and thus have no actual timekeeping function.

Colour Plate 29 shows another typically Chinese market clock in a cupola topped gilt case. It has an unsigned quarter striking and musical three train fusée and chain movement. Quarters are struck on two bells and one of two tunes is played every hour or at will on eight bells. The backplate is engraved with flowers and scrolling leaves. The clock stands 15 inches high. It has verge escapement, sweep centre seconds and an enamel dial. The paste jewels that decorate the dial are another usual Chinese market feature. The clock can be dated *circa* 1790.

Colour Plate 30 illustrates an example of another type of Chinese market clock that differs from the two examples just shown, in that although the movement and dial were made in Britain *circa* 1820 the case is thought to have been made in China. Properly speaking it is perhaps outside the scope of this book but increasingly during the early nineteenth century English movements were cased in China. Eventually a stage was reached when entire (and often very complicated) clocks were made in China. Cases made in China were not, as a general rule, as well made and finished as those made in England, where casemaking had always been of a very high standard but there can be no doubt that the more elaborate Chinese cases look extremely effective. The movements too were well made, though not finished to the same standard as the English examples.

It is interesting to reflect that the later Chinese market clocks had gone full circle. They had started by being made in England in styles which London clockmakers thought would appeal to the Chinese. They finished by being made in China as copies of those earlier English attempts to create a Chinese taste in clocks that had in reality never existed.

It would be invidious to show further examples of Chinese market clocks. They are seldom seen for sale in England and are not particularly to the English taste. Care should be taken however not to confuse Chinese made clocks, which are often housed in padoukwood or hardwood cases and sometimes bear English 'nonsense' signatures, with contemporary English clocks.

Clocks made for export were an important part of the London clock trade. The willingness of London clockmakers and casemakers to produce work which was excitingly different and versatile redounds much to their credit. It does much to explain their enormous success and the considerable status achieved by the London trade during the period under review.

PLATE V/16 *Unsigned but attributed to Cox. Silver and blue enamel clock. Chinese market.* Circa *1790.*

COLOUR PLATE 31 *Benbow. Newport. Shropshire: Unusual provincial bracket clock with lunar feature and alarum.* Circa *1805*

COLOUR PLATE 30 *(left) Unsigned. English movement with elaborate automata. Clock case made in China for the Chinese market.* Circa *1820.*

CHAPTER SIX
The Georgian Period 1800-1830

An examination of a large number of bracket clocks made between 1800 and 1830 reveals that two different types of clock were being made, often by the same makers. The first type, mostly made during the first twenty years of the nineteenth century, consists of clocks that are a natural progression from the clocks that were being made during the last years of the eighteenth century. They include bell-top, break-arch and the arch-top clocks that had started to become popular towards the end of the eighteenth century. Inevitably there are also a few clocks which are difficult to classify precisely. These have been included in the section which looks most suitable. The second type, which started to appear *circa* 1805, consists of examples that are different because they are particularly Regency in appearance, that is to say they exhibit many of the characteristics which distinguish what we now call the Regency Style of furniture. In fact the Regency lasted only from 1811 until 1820 but the second phase of the neo-classical style of furniture, which had been dominant in Europe since the mid-eighteenth century, commenced *circa* 1800 and lasted until about 1830, the end of the Georgian period. The Regency style denotes the English version of this classical revival as it applies to both furniture and decor. Its roots were earlier, though it owes its name to the Prince Regent who, on coming of age in 1785, commissioned Henry Holland (1745-1806) to rebuild and refurbish Carlton House. Henry Holland had married the daughter of Capability Brown, the famous landscape gardener and was later in partnership with him.

Henry Holland was in tune with the new movement and was a great promoter of it. He carried out many important commissions for members of the ruling class of the day. The Prince Regent, George IV as he subsequently became, was a lavish patron of the movement. If we liken the new movement to an orchestra, then the Prince Regent was the patron and Henry Holland was the principal conductor of many important orchestras. But the most influential composer was Thomas Hope (1768-1831). Hope was the author of *Household Furniture and Interior Decoration executed from Designs by Thomas Hope*. It was published in 1807.

Holland and Hope are the principal names associated with the Regency style but, just as the style itself drew its inspiration from many classical sources and styles, Greek, Roman, Egyptian, Etruscan, Chinese, French and Gothic, so too there were many other people who contributed to it during the last years of the eighteenth century and the first thirty years of the nineteenth century. Among them were Sheraton who, in his *Cabinet-Maker and Upholsterer's Drawing*

Book, 1791-1794, bridged the gap between the early Hepplewhite interpretation of Adam's classical ideas by emphasising delicacy of form. Sheraton's last book, *The Cabinet Maker, Upholsterer and General Artist's Encyclopaedia, 1804-1806,* was the first to illustrate the Egyptian taste, a recurring theme of the Regency style. Thomas Tatham (1772-1842) who was employed by Holland to visit the Mediterranean and provide him with drawings of classical ornaments, published, in 1799, *Etchings of Ancient Ornamental Architecture Drawn from the Originals in Rome and Other Parts of Italy.* There were subsequent editions, including one at Weimar in 1805. In 1806 he published *Etchings. Representing Fragments of Grecian and Roman Architectural Ornament.* There were other publications. To Tatham must go the credit for much of the detail ornamentation of Regency furniture, but if it was Hope who classified and codified the Regency style it was the cabinetmaker George Smith, whose pattern book *A collection of Designs for Household Furniture and Interior Decoration,* published in 1808, popularised the style and brought it to the attention of the growing new wealthy middle classes. Another cabinetmaker who was a pioneer of the Regency style was George Bullock, the man whose style dominated fashionable furniture design in the years after Waterloo.[1] Bullock died in 1818.

Regency design and decor was not without its detractors. This, presumably, is why there were two styles of clock made during the Regency, which for all practical purposes covers the period 1800-30 under review. Clearly and indeed sensibly, the fashionable and leading clockmakers of the day hedged their bets. If the customer wanted a clock made to one of the new designs then so be it. If something traditional was sought, then it too was available. By the standards of today this attitude is no more than prudent business sense. But to the clockmaker of the early nineteenth century, steeped in two and a half centuries of tradition and conservatism, it was a dramatic volte-face.

The move towards clocks that could be seen purely as functional pieces of fashionable furniture has already been noted. By the end of the first decade of the nineteenth century the transition was effectively complete. The clockmaker was no longer the dominant partner in the design and manufacture of the bracket clock. No matter how beautifully he made and finished his movement it was now taken completely for granted. The bracket clock-buying public wanted clocks that told the time, for that was their function, but the clock now had also to be an integral part of the decor chosen by the customers and interior designers of the day. The difference between the new distinctive Regency styles and the more traditional production can be seen clearly if the two types are illustrated and discussed separately, but both styles will be seen to share the same types of dials, hands and movements. During this period verge escapements became increasingly rare and backplates were becoming increasingly plain, though border engraving was common enough. Some anchor escapement pendulums were also lightly engraved, sometimes in conjunction with a simple form of micrometer adjustment above the bob. Presumably these refinements were optional extras. The case materials popular during the eighteenth century continued in use but were joined by

1 Bryan Reade quoted in *English Furniture. 1800-1851,* E.T. Joy. This book was used as the main source material for the summary of the background of the Regency style and for many of the subsequent details provided.

COLOUR PLATE 32 *Grimalde and Johnson. Rare mulberry wood lancet timepiece ornamented with dragons and Greek keying. Circa 1820.*

COLOUR PLATE 33 *Robert Roskell. Liverpool. A Regency bracket clock in the Graeco-Egyptian taste in the manner of George Bullock. It contains a musical box in the base. Circa 1815.*

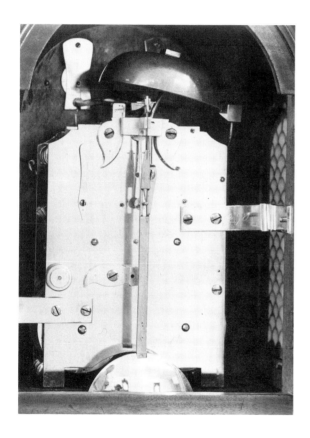

PLATE VI/1 *Dwerrihouse and Carter. Early nineteenth century mahogany break-arch clock in the tradition of the late eighteenth century.* Circa *1805.*

PLATE VI/2 *Plain backplate of the Dwerrihouse and Carter clock shown in Plate VI/I. Anchor escapement and shouldered and footed plates.*

rosewood. Rosewood had been used in marquetry longcases at the end of the seventeenth century and was now re-introduced.

Traditional Style Bracket Clocks 1800-1830

The Dwerrihouse and Carter break-arch mahogany bracket clock illustrated in Plates VI/1 and VI/2 looks at first sight to be a typical late eighteenth century example. The case, dial and fittings could all have been made at any time between 1780 and the end of the century. There are four features that place this clock firmly in the nineteenth century. The first is that the partnership of Dwerrihouse and Carter appears to have commenced in 1800. They remained in or near Berkeley Square until 1827, when the partnership ended. Second, the hands are of a style that is not seen before the nineteenth century; they are certainly original. Third, the clock has anchor escapement and a plain

PLATE VI/3 *Allam and Caithness. Plain silvered dial plate and hands typical of traditional early nineteenth century bracket clocks. Circa 1805.*

PLATE VI/4 *The border engraved backplate of the Allam and Caithness clock shown in Plate VI/3.*

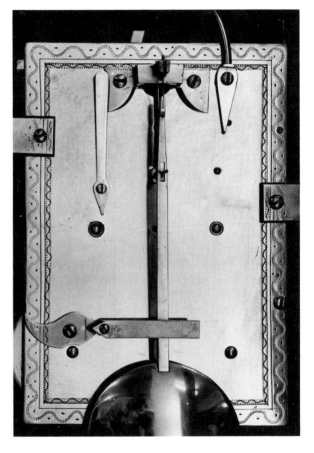

backplate. Fourth, the diamond-shaped white bone inlaid key escutcheon is an often-found feature on clock cases of the 1800-30 period. These four features taken together suggest a date of manufacture of between 1800 and 1810.

Allam and Caithness were the makers of the simpler break-arch mahogany bracket clock illustrated in Plates VI/3 and VI/4. This clock also exhibits four features which allow us to date the clock *circa* 1805. The first is the maker's name. The partnership of Allam and Caithness ran from 1800-09. Second, it will be seen that the dial is now a plain silvered brass sheet with no engraved corner spandrels. Plain silvered dials such as this were not unknown in the late eighteenth century but here they are used in conjunction with hands of a type usually seen early in the nineteenth century, though they had begun to appear

in the last years of the eighteenth century. Third, the movement has anchor escapement. The border engraving of the backplate is typical of early nineteenth century clocks. Fourth, the case door is fitted with a white bone key escutcheon.

The Dwerrihouse and Carter break-arch clock shown in Plate VI/1 and VI/2 was an example of a nineteenth century clock in which silvered chapter plates were fitted to an engraved polished and lacquered brass dial plate. The large mahogany bracket clock by Biddell of London shown in Plate VI/5 is fitted with a similar dial plate on which are mounted enamel dials. This is a clock which betrays its early nineteenth century date by its Arabic numerals, its hands and its anchor escapement. The clocks shown in Plates IV/52 and

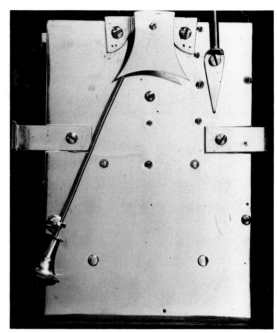

PLATE VI/6 *William Payne. Traditional break-arch case but the engraved and silvered dial shows a fine mix of late eighteenth and early nineteenth century features. Circa 1810.*

PLATE VI/7 *The backplate of the William Payne clock shown in Plate VI/6. In spite of its* circa *1810 date this clock was made with verge escapement.*

IV/87, by Chancellor and Dunkley, were very early examples of Georgian clocks with Arabic numerals. Most of them occur 1800-30. But in many respects, this is a clock that could have been made ten or fifteen years earlier. These overlapping styles are equally evident in the clock by William Payne of London shown in Plate VI/6. Here the hands and numerals are what would be expected in the early nineteenth century, as is the plain backplate, Plate VI/7. Yet the verge escapement, dotted minutes and engraved dial centre would have been equally at home during the last years of the eighteenth century. In fact this clock was probably made *circa* 1810.

Some idea of the range and variety of traditional quarter chiming and musical clocks available during the early part of the nineteenth century can be gained by examining the seven examples illustrated in Plates VI/8-14.

Plate VI/8 shows a quarter chiming mahogany clock in an elaborated arch-top case by John Thwaites, London. The silvered dial is numbered 2704. The backplate, which is engraved with leaves and flowers, is also signed and numbered. The clock has anchor escapement and chimes the quarters on eight bells. The hour is struck on a ninth bell. John Thwaites' number, 2704, suggests a date *circa* 1802. It will be noted that the subsidiary chapter ring for the control of the striking is engraved 'Strike and Silent' yet the clock is

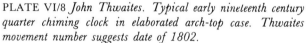

PLATE VI/8 *John Thwaites. Typical early nineteenth century quarter chiming clock in elaborated arch-top case. Thwaites movement number suggests date of 1802.*

PLATE VI/9 *Robert Roskell. Liverpool. Musical clock. Cream painted dial. Bell-top turntable case. Thwaites movement number suggests date of 1802.*

described as a chiming clock. Generally speaking any quarter striking clock that strikes the quarters on four or more bells can be described as a quarter chiming clock. Clocks that strike the quarters on less than four bells are simply quarter striking clocks. It seems to have been the rather confusing practice to indicate the on/off of the music of Georgian musical clocks by using the words chime and silent. Musical clocks such as those shown in Plates V1/9 and VI/10 can be seen to be fitted with on/off controls for both the hourly strike and the music. Four train clocks and grande sonnerie clocks usually have on/off controls for all their different functions.

The strike/silent subsidiary indication, top right on the dial of Thwaites' clock number 2704 controls the hour striking and the quarters. The subsidiary indication, top left, is for the days of the month. The hands are gilt, a fashionable finish at the time, but modelled somewhat in the manner that was fashionable about twenty years earlier. The clock stands 25½ inches high.

The musical bell-top mahogany clock signed on its cream painted dial 'Robert Roskell Liverpool', Plate VI/9, is another Thwaites production. It is

PLATE VI/10 *Wood. Musical clock in satinwood case with many 'Sheraton' features. Painted dial probably made in Birmingham. Circa 1800.*

numbered 2655 and is thought to have been supplied to Robert Roskell in 1802. As can be seen there is a choice of twelve tunes. These are played on twelve bells. This is an imposing clock standing 36 inches high. The bell-top case is fitted with Corinthian capitals and a cupola top surmounted by a cast metal figure. The case is of the turntable variety.

The musical bell-top clock shown in Plate VI/10 is even taller than Robert Roskell's clock. It stands 39 inches high. The very fine case is of satinwood with kingwood bandings. It is inlaid with swags, husks and fan medallions and has Corinthian corner columns. The sides of the case are inlaid with baskets of fruit and country scenes. The dial is painted and has flower decorated corners. It was probably made in Birmingham. The date is shown round the inside of the chapter ring. There is a choice of eight tunes played on twelve bells. The pin barrel is at right angles to the back of the clock. The maker, Wood of London, is believed to have had a considerable export business but the dial and case of this clock suggest it was made for the home market. It is possible that the movement was made by Thwaites, as were so many musical clocks of this era. The clock can be dated *circa* 1800.

The three pad arch-top mahogany quarter striking clock shown in Plate VI/11 was made between 1800 and 1810. The hands are similar to those of the Dwerrihouse and Carter clock in Plate VI/1. The silvered dial is completely plain. It will be seen that the dial plate is secured by screws. Silvered dial plates were secured to the dial feet by any one of three methods: rivetting, screw threaded from the rear, i.e. the front of the dial foot is made with a small screw, or screwed from the front, as in this instance. The Perigals were a well-known clockmaking family during the 1741-1840 period.

PLATE VI/11 *Perigal. Quarter chiming full arch dial, mahogany three pad break-arch case. Completely plain engraved silvered dial secured to dial pillars by small screws.* Circa *1805.*

PLATE VI/12 *Grant. Quarter striking clock in elaborated mahogany break-arch case. Dial and case with many late eighteenth century features.* Circa *1805.*

PLATE VI/13 *Evill. Bath. Musical clock in elaborated break-arch mahogany case. Painted dial. Decorative, typically Regency, lion's mask handles. Circa 1815.*

PLATE VI/14 *Parkinson and Frodsham. Quarter chiming clock in elaborated break-arch case inlaid with brass stringing and stars, both Regency features. Plain white painted dial. Decorative ring handles. Circa 1815.*

Plate VI/12 shows a 24 inch high quarter striking clock by Grant, number 269. Surprisingly for such a large clock the quarter striking employs only two bells. Perhaps the clock was made for boardroom or office use. A quarter chime of several bells might have proved distracting. The case, save for the ivory key escutcheon, exhibits a fine mixture of late eighteenth century features. The brass dial plate is fitted with enamel dials. The hands are the latest visible feature of this clock. They are typically early nineteenth century. The backplate of the movement has border engraving and anchor escapement is fitted. The clock probably dates *circa* 1805.

The clocks shown in Plates VI/13 and VI/14 are sufficiently traditional in appearance to be included in this traditional early nineteenth century section, but both also exhibit Regency features. The clock by Evill and Son of Bath, Plate VI/13, can be seen to have ring handles. These are mounted in pressed brass lion masks, a particularly Regency design first noted in Sheraton's *Cabinet Dictionary* of 1803. Handles such as these are noteworthy for another reason. They lack strength, i.e. they are really only for ornament. Eventually,

PLATE VI/15 *(right) George Grove. Small arch-top mahogany case with brass furniture and opening bezel. This arch-top case style remained popular for many years. Gilt hands. Circa 1805.*

PLATE VI/16 *Thomas Pace. Break-arch mahogany case veneered in contrasting panels. Reeded pillars. Opening bezel. Traditional carrying handles. Circa 1810.*

as we shall see, many late Georgian clocks will be made without handles or with handles that are largely decorative. The case of this clock stands 23 inches high. The movement is musical. Five tunes are available played on fourteen bells. The dial is painted. The gilt tear-drop hands have an additional chain link design feature often seen on Regency clocks. The clock dates *circa* 1815.

Parkinson and Frodsham's full arch painted dial quarter chiming clock, Plate VI/14, is also fitted with ring handles but two more Regency features are the inlaid brass stars in the case door and the use of brass stringing. Joy[2] suggests a French origin for the brass star. It appears in Hope's *Household Furniture* and was used by Smith. Ebony inlay is another typical Regency feature.

The break-arch cases which were joined by the arch-top cases early in the

2 *English Furniture 1800-1851*, E.T. Joy.

PLATE VI/17 *Grant. Unusual satinwood case with architectural front and opening bezel. 'Neo-Grec' side volutes. Grant made many clocks in similar cases.* Circa *1810*.

nineteenth century both continued to be very popular until the end of the Georgian period but in addition to Regency details such as those just described there were a number of other variations and detail changes. Perhaps the most obvious was that many clocks were made in which only the bezel rather than the whole of the case front door opened to reveal the dial. This is, of course, a feature that we have already seen on eighteenth century balloon clocks where the opening bezel was necessary to avoid upsetting the line of the case. The opening bezel suffers from one disadvantage; namely that a heavy cast bezel can eventually break the hinge that connects it to the case. Three examples of clocks with opening bezels are shown in Plates VI/15-17. Each is a typical early nineteenth century clock of the more traditional type. Each shows further variations in style and detail.

Plate VI/15 shows a neat arch-top clock of small size by George Grove. It has a border engraved circular movement, an enamel dial, gilt hands and Arabic numerals. The recessed panel below the dial and the front of the case are brass bound. The keyhole for the brass bezel is in the side of the case. This

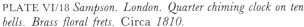

PLATE VI/18 *Sampson. London. Quarter chiming clock on ten bells. Brass floral frets.* Circa *1810.*

PLATE VI/19 *Whitehurst. Derby. The whole front door of this mahogany case, a variation of the break-arch, opens to reveal the painted dial. Quarter chiming clock on eight bells. Brass fish-scale frets.* Circa *1810.*

clock was made *circa* 1805. Thomas Pace's clock, Plate VI/16, also has gilt hands and a painted dial. The movement is scratch signed within by William Robson. William Robson signed clocks in his own name but was also a well-known wholesale manufacturer to the trade. His output included musical clocks. He was Master of the Clockmakers' Company in 1817 and 1819. His work, like that of Thwaites and Reed and Handley and Moore, another manufacturer who made many clocks for the trade, is always of high quality. The case of Pace's clock is also of fine quality with good brass mounts and some use of line inlay and contrasting mahogany veneers. Plate VI/17 illustrates a satinwood clock by Grant of Fleet Street, number 382. The full arch case has an unusual architectural front and side volutes. Cescinsky and Webster illustrate a similar clock in *English Domestic Clocks.* They describe the side volutes as being Neo-Grec in design. Grant made many clocks similar to this in various sizes. This example was made perhaps a few years later than the Grant clock shown in Plate VI/12.

Plate VI/18 shows yet another variation of the break-arch case design.

Curiously this is a design that looks better in a photograph than in the flesh. In the flesh the design appears nearly top-heavy. This is a good quality clock made by Sampson of London *circa* 1810. It is quarter chiming on ten bells. The attractive floral sound frets are made of brass. The clock stands 20 inches high. The hands are of the moonpoise design. Another example of this case style, with a full opening front door, is shown in Plate VI/19. This example is also quarter chiming, but on eight bells and is smaller. The height is 17½ inches. The sound frets are of the fish-scale variety. The maker is Whitehurst of Derby. Cescinsky and Webster illustrate a similar clock in *English Domestic Clocks*.

The cases of the two clocks shown in Plates VI/20 and VI/21 are made from Paperware, a mixture of pulped paper, glue and chalk which was pressed, moulded and baked into a hard material that could be treated like wood.[3] This was a form of papier mâché, a substance which was made originally in Persia and the East and reached Britain via France acquiring the name en route, in the seventeenth century. Henry Clay patented the type of papier mâché used in these clock cases in 1772. He called his product Paperware. It was used to make many domestic products and when painted, varnished and polished was even used for coach panels. It has not been possible to trace Strickland and Richardson, the 'makers' of the break-sided type balloon Paperware timepiece shown in Plate VI/20, but the movement appears to be of good quality. The backplate is engraved with an urn. The pendulum bob is engraved with a flowerhead. The clock stands 13½ inches high and is decorated with a fine musical trophy and sprigs of flowers. The second Paperware clock, Plate VI/21, is unsigned. It stands 16 inches high and is decorated with flowers with a floral trophy in the middle of the front of the case. The movement is of good quality. Both clocks date *circa* 1810. Presumably the movements for these cases were bought in from the wholesale clock trade and it may be that Strickland and Richardson were furniture retailers.

The timepiece by Johnson, Strand, London, Plate VI/22, is of interest because the case is of a style that is particularly associated with this maker, who was in partnership with Grimalde from 1810 until 1825. There are brass lines and star inlays in the sides of the case. The unusual handle is of a style associated with these two makers. It will be seen that a heavy cast-silvered brass bezel is fitted within the thickness of the case door. Both Nicholls[4] and the writer have observed that a case style not dissimilar to this version of the break-arch was used in Dublin at the end of the eighteenth century. Johnson's clock dates *circa* 1830 and is only 9¼ inches high. Three more clocks by Grimalde and Johnson are shown in Plates VI/23, 24 and 25.

As was explained earlier, Georgian bracket clocks are generally very much of the London school in appearance. But occasionally clocks are found, usually from remote areas, that are decidedly provincial in appearance. Colour Plate 31 shows a clock by Benbow of Newport in Shropshire that probably dates *circa* 1805. The painted dial has a lunar feature and alarum work is fitted to the movement. The bell-top case is veneered in mahogany with satinwood around the arch and a yew wood veneered door. There are inlaid lines of boxwood and ebony. French feet are fitted in the manner of some provincial painted dial

3 *English Furniture. 1800-1851*, E.T. Joy. For a fuller description of the history of papier mâché.
4 *English Bracket and Mantel Clocks*, Andrew Nicholls.

PLATE VI/20 *Strickland and Richardson. Timepiece balloon clock in decorated Paperware case. Paperware was a form of papier mâché.* Circa *1810.*

PLATE VI/21 *Unsigned. Another decorated Paperware clock.* Circa *1810.*

longcase clocks of the period. Plate VI/28 illustrates another unusual provincial painted dial bracket clock in a mahogany case with Sheraton shell inlays. It was made by E. Drakeford of Congleton in Cheshire *circa* 1815.

Late Georgian Clocks with pronounced Regency characteristics

The late Georgian clocks discussed this far have been the natural successors to their late eighteenth century progenitors. The clocks which will be discussed in the sequence that follows all show more pronounced Regency characteristics, often combining classical, including Egyptian, Chinese and Greek influences, with English neo-classicism, Empire and Gothic Revival to produce clock cases that are at once distinctive and in some instances extremely elegant.

PLATE VI/22 *(above) W. Johnson. Very small ebonised clock, 9¼ in. (23.5cm) high. Case style often associated with the partnership of Grimalde and Johnson. Unusual handle and heavy cast bezel fitted to traditional door. Plain silvered dial. Circa 1830.*

PLATE VI/23 *(above right) Grimalde and Johnson. Small ebonised break-arch clock, 10in. (25.4cm) high. Plain silvered dial. Good snake hands. Acorn feet. Circa 1820.*

PLATE VI/24 *(right) Grimalde and Johnson. Ebonised break-arch case. The pull wind for the alarum is mounted on the top right hand side. Circa 1820.*

PLATE VI/25 (above left) Grimalde and Johnson. Small time-piece ebonised break-arch clock, 9¾ in (24.8cm) high. Pull wind alarum. Plain silvered dial. Acorn feet. Circa 1825.

PLATE VI/26 (left) Thos. Richards. Typical break-arch mahogany case of a type first used late eighteenth century. Early nineteenth century give-away features are diamond key escutcheon and snake hands. Circa 1805.

PLATE VI/27 (above) I. Dodds. Mahogany break-sided balloon clock of basically late eighteenth century design. Early nineteenth century give-away feature is chequered stringing. Fine inlaid musical trophy. Circa 1810.

PLATE VI/28 *E. Drakeford.*
Congleton. Cheshire. Unusual
mahogany provincial clock.
Normally provincial bracket
clocks follow London styles.
This is an exception.
Circa *1815.*

The clock illustrated in Plate VI/30, a gadroon top mahogany example made *circa* 1810 by James McCabe, Royal Exchange, London, is predominantly Egyptian in style though the side sound apertures and brass frets incline toward the Gothic. Scholars had always been interested in Egyptian design; the palmette, anthemion, obelisk, sphinx and pyramid were already familiar details of classical, if mainly architectural, decoration, but public interest in things Egyptian was stimulated by the Napoleonic expedition of 1798. Napoleon's entourage included many savants who subsequently published

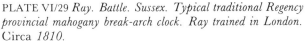

PLATE VI/29 *Ray. Battle. Sussex. Typical traditional Regency provincial mahogany break-arch clock. Ray trained in London.* Circa *1810.*

PLATE VI/30 *James McCabe. Gothic sound apertures, gadroon top, but Egyptian influence predominates. Mahogany case. Pineapple brass finial.* Circa *1810.*

their findings, indeed Dominique-Vivant Denon's *Voyage dans la basse et la haute Egypte* published in 1802 was translated into English the same year. Dominique-Vivant Denon was an archaeologist who later became director-general of the French Museums. Public interest in things Egyptian was further whetted by Nelson's dramatic defeat of the French fleet at the battle of the Nile.

Furniture in the Egyptian style was first illustrated in Britain by Sheraton in his *Encyclopaedia* of 1804-06. It was popularised by Smith's *Household Furniture* of 1808. Plates VI/31, VI/32 and VI/33 show clocks of the same genre as the clock in Plate VI/30 though the lancet top case of the clock shown in Plate VI/33 is Gothic in outline. The paw feet are a Sheraton feature often found on Regency clocks. It will be noticed that three out of four of these clocks were made without handles.

There was a revival of interest in chinoiserie during the Regency period. Chinese designs for European lacquerwork had been popular for both furniture and clock cases until nearly the end of the eighteenth century, indeed lacquered bracket clock cases continued to occur in the nineteenth century, but this was nearly always a matter of Eastern decoration rather than form. Just a few eighteenth century bracket clocks were made with pagoda tops and the pagoda top, albeit a thoroughly anglicised variation, was absorbed into classic

PLATE VI/31 *Unsigned. Another clock of the same genre as Plate VI/30. Acroteria finials. Paw feet were another popular Regency feature. Acorn finial perhaps a replacement. Circa 1810.*

PLATE VI/32 *(below left) Barwise. Yet another clock in the Egyptian taste. Acroteria finials. Circa 1815.*

PLATE VI/33 *(below) Unsigned. Gothic mahogany lancet top case in the Egyptian taste. Paw feet. Circa 1815.*

198

PLATE VI/34 *Grignion. Regency Gothic lancet top case with chinoiserie influence. The case pillars are of simulated bamboo. Circa 1810.*

PLATE VI/35 *(above) Sinderby. Another typical Regency Gothic lancet top case. Satinwood with brass mounts. Circa 1815.*

PLATE VI/36 *(left) Thomas Moss. Typical Regency Gothic lancet top case. Lion's mask handles. Circa 1810.*

longcase clock design, but although a small number of longcase clocks are made which are fairly Chinese in form 'Chinese Chippendale' should not be confused with applied Chinese decoration which was the feature of so many eighteenth century lacquered clock cases and movement backplate engravings.

The clock by Grignion of London, illustrated in Plate VI/34 is of the lancet top form with simulated bamboo columns fitted to the front of the case. Apart from the Chinese influence of the front columns it is a typical lancet top clock of the period. Simulated bamboo columns are fitted to a number of lancet top clocks, the design lends itself to this treatment but, generally speaking, Chinese design was applied to very few bracket clock cases.

Colour Plate 32 shows a mulberry wood lancet top timepiece by Grimalde and Johnson. It has acorn feet, a milled bezel, Greek key decoration and an ebony inlay of two dragons. There is also a brass and ebony inlay beneath the lancet top. The hands are of the moonpoise design. It can be dated *circa* 1820.

The lancet top clock by Sinderby of London shown in Plate VI/35 has alarum work and a satinwood case with applied brass ornamentation. Once again the side frets are Gothic in style. The ornamental handles appear to be of the lion's head design. This clock, too, can be dated *circa* 1815.

The last lancet top clock to be shown, Plate VI/36, is a simpler clock in an ebonised case with applied brass ornamentation. The ornamental handles are of lion's head design. This clock was made by Thomas Moss of London, *circa* 1810.

Clocks of French design appeared occasionally throughout the Georgian era. The lyre-shaped case is a French design that was used from time to time during the Regency period. The example illustrated in Plate VI/37 has a fine solidly English looking mahogany case which makes much use of applied ornamentation. The base once contained a musical box whose operation would have been tripped by the clock movement. The bezel is milled and gilded. The dial is painted. This clock was made by James McCabe *circa* 1815. The second lyre-shaped clock, Plate VI/38 has a case that undoubtedly emanated from the same source. It contains a movement by Loudon of London. The dial is silvered. The hands are of the attractive chain link moon-poise design.

The chamfer top case and its derivatives were an integral part of the Regency scene. They could be said to typify all that is best in classic Regency clock case design. The mahogany cased example by Gravell and Son, London, shown in Plate VI/39, has gilded brass cornucopia handles and is surmounted by a gilded pineapple. The dial is silvered, fairly unusual for a chamfer top clock, most of them have painted dials. The date is shown, again an unusual feature in clocks of this period. The hands are particularly delicate. This clock dates *circa* 1815. The clock shown in Plate VI/40 is cased in rosewood which was much used for pure Regency clocks and was, of course, extensively used for Regency furniture. Brass inlay makes an effective contrast with rosewood. In addition to the brass plate beneath the pineapple, brass is used to define the spandrel corner panels which in turn are inlaid with brass. Brass is also used to trim the front corners of the case. There is an inlaid rectangle of brass stringing in the base. Brass ball feet are another particular feature found on

PLATE VI/37 *(left) James McCabe. Mahogany lyre-shaped case in the English tradition but of French design. The base once contained a musical box.* Circa *1815.*

PLATE VI/38 *(right) Loudon. Another mahogany lyre-shaped case of French design. Cases of French design appear throughout the Georgian period.* Circa *1825.*

early nineteenth century cases. This clock was made *circa* 1820.

The chamfer top case continued to be made long after the end of the Georgian era but a popular alternative, the gadroon top, started to appear towards the end of the Georgian period. The gadroon top ebonised clock by Alexander Purvis shown in Plate VI/41 dates *circa* 1825. The brass side frets of this clock are Gothic. The classic architectural and functional simplicity of the original chamfer top case was sufficiently confident to allow several variations and developments which in no way weaken the elegance of the basic design. Soon we find examples such as the Moorish arch-topped case door shown in Plate VI/42. It is used in conjunction with a cast brass bezel fitted within the thickness of the case door. Both dial and bezel are silvered. The case

PLATE VI/39 *Gravell and Son. Classic Regency elegance. Chamfer top mahogany case. Circa 1815.*

PLATE VI/40 *W.T. Tyas. A variation in rosewood of the chamfer top case. Much use of brass. Circa 1820.*

PLATE VI/41 *Alex Purvis. The gadroon top was a variation of the chamfer top. Circa 1825.*

PLATE VI/42 *G. Searle.*
Rosewood case with gadroon
top. Moorish arch shape to
front door. Plain silvered dial.
Circa *1830.*

has a gadroon top and is made of rosewood. This clock was made by G. Searle of London *circa* 1830.

Three further variations are shown in in Plates VI/43, VI/44 and VI/45. The hands of the rosewood example by Wyatt and the ebonised example by Denne, Plates VI/43 and VI/45, are particularly delicate. They are of a design that starts to appear right at the end of the Georgian period. The Denne clock introduces another feature which starts to appear at this time, namely the fully engraved dial plate on which is mounted an enamel dial. This is evidently very fine and expensive work. Another fully engraved dial plate is shown in Plate VI/46. Here it is used in conjunction with a full arch dial. These four clocks all date *circa* 1830.

But what of break-arch and arch-top Regency clocks? They too are well represented. Plate VI/47 shows a brass inlaid rosewood example by Litherland Davies of Liverpool, *circa* 1820. The case is a flattened break-arch variation

PLATE VI/43 *Wyatt. Another typical late Regency gadroon topped rosewood case. Brass inlay. Excellent hands. Circa 1830.*

PLATE VI/44 *Frodsham. Rosewood case of a design that is a variation of the basic chamfer top often used for small clocks usually of high quality. Circa 1830.*

PLATE VI/45 *(left) John Denne. Engraved dial plates used in conjunction with enamel dials started to appear about this time. Circa 1830.*

PLATE VI/46 *Barwise. Small gadroon topped clock with enamel dial and engraved gilt dial plate. Circa 1830.*

PLATE VI/47 *Litherland Davies. Liverpool. Rosewood caddy topped brass inlaid case of flattened break-arch design. Circa 1820.*

based perhaps on the dials of this shape first made nearly three quarters of a century earlier. The caddy top is surmounted by a pineapple.

Another break-arch design which was much used for smaller clocks is shown in Plate VI/48. It is a mahogany cased example by Arnold of London. The Greek keying, use of ebony inlay and the paw feet are all classic Regency features. These elegant small clocks usually had plain sides inlaid with ebony stringing and brass flower heads. The design is clearly visible on the sides of the similar clock by Grimalde and Johnson shown in Plate VI/49. In fact the Grimalde and Johnson clock is rather larger than the norm for this design. It quarter chimes on eight bells. No doubt it is for this reason that fish-scale side frets were fitted. Both these clocks date *circa* 1825.

The four clocks illustrated in Plates VI/50-53 are typical Regency arch-top designs. The smallest of them, Plate VI/50, is a rosewood example by James Tupman of Great Russell Street, Bloomsbury, London, which stands only 13 inches high. As already noted, these smaller Regency cases were often made without handles. Many Regency clocks have painted or enamel dials, but the design of Tupman's clock lends itself to the traditional engraved silvered brass dial. The clock by William Chater, London, Plate VI/51, and that by Robert Cook, London, shown in Plate VI/52 (the name is lost from the dial but is engraved within a cartouche on the backplate) both possess mahogany arch dial cases in which the appearance is varied by the use of spandrel corners. The Robert Cook clock spandrels are of satinwood. In addition there are ovals of satinwood inlay. Both these clocks were made *circa* 1815. The last of this series, the mahogany clock by Manders of Windsor, Plate VI/53, features brass inlay and brass trim. It also has a reeded moulding round the base and around the top of the surround. This detail is often seen on Regency clocks. It is found

PLATE VI/48 *Arnold. Regency mahogany break-arch case design sometimes used for smaller Regency clocks. Ebony inlay. Greek keying and paw feet are classically Regency features. Circa 1825.*

PLATE VI/49 *Grimalde and Johnson. Slightly larger quarter chiming version of the break-arch case shown in Plate VI/48. Circa 1825.*

PLATE VI/50 *James Tupman. Small arch-top rosewood case with brass binding and inlay. No handles.* Circa *1825.*

PLATE VI/51 *(right) W. Chater. Elaborated mahogany arch-top case with inlaid brass spandrel corners.* Circa *1815.*

most often perhaps on the chamfer top designs. This moulding, usually ebonised, was produced by a labour-saving technique that was cheaper than carving. It is referred to by Cescinksy and Webster as a typically English Empire or late Sheraton detail.

Many Regency clocks were made which were variations on those illustrated but enough examples have been shown for the reader to recognise the style.

A lyre-shaped clock that contained a musical box has already been shown but Colour Plate 33 illustrates another clock containing a musical box that epitomises the Regency taste. The catalogue description when it was sold by Christie's merits reprinting in full:

'...An imposing Regency mahogany and ebonised musical bracket clock in the manner of George Bullock in the Graeco-Egyptian taste, the two part case on ball feet with pediment-topped quoined broad plinth narrowing via palmette fronted baluster scrolls to gadrooned chamfer top ''clock'' case with glazed eight inch circular painted dial signed Robt Roskell Liverpool between reeded tampered angles headed by acroteria, brass tracery silk frets, the twin chain fusée movement with hour strike on bell, anchor escapement, micrometer pendulum with screw holdfast, repeat signature on the border engraved shaped backplate, securing brackets to the case, trip linkage to the chain fusée musical movement in the base playing six tunes from a one and a half inch

PLATE VI/52 *Robert Cook. Mahogany arch-top case with panels of satinwood and plain and chequered line inlay. Circa 1815.*

PLATE VI/53 *Manders. Windsor. Elaborated mahogany arch-top case with brass inlay and ebonised reeded moulding that is a typically late 'Sheraton' detail. Circa 1820.*

diameter pin barrel on thirteen and a half inch comb with individually anchored teeth. Twenty nine inches high.

Footnote: Although no documented clock by Bullock, (1783-1818) cabinet maker of Liverpool and later London, has been identified, the present clock is very markedly in his style. For examples of his work see 1988 exhibition catalogue, George Bullock, Cabinet-maker, edited by Clive Wainwright.'

This is a fitting clock with which to conclude a survey of one hundred and sixteen years of superlative English clockmaking.

CHAPTER SEVEN

Restoration and Purchase

At the time of writing (1991), the oldest Georgian bracket clocks are 277 years old. The youngest are 161 years old. It is only to be expected that all of them will show signs of the various natural and unnatural experiences they will have undergone during their long lives. Among the natural experiences can be counted moving house on several occasions, with the knocks and bangs attendant upon such upheavals. All of them will have made several visits to the clockmaker, albeit probably at too infrequent intervals. Some of the men who have cleaned, oiled, silvered chapter rings, bushed, replaced broken springs and repaired broken hands will have been experts at their work. But others will have been itinerant Victorian clock jobbers who will have bodged it. Many clocks will have been converted from verge to anchor escapement. At the time this was considered a worthwhile exercise because an anchor escapement gives better timekeeping. It was also a lucrative task for the clockmaker. A good number of earlier clocks that were fitted with pull-quarter repeating work will have had their repeating work removed by incompetent repairers who did not understand the mechanism and were concerned only with making stopped clocks go.

These clocks are the lucky ones. Their less fortunate brethren may have been dropped, with disastrous effects on their cases and probably severe damage to their movements. Some will have had their movements repaired and their cases patched up and will have been returned to service but other movements, their cases beyond repair, will have been consigned to attics and outbuildings. Among this latter class there will also be many movements whose cases were lost by fire or the bombs of two world wars.

There is another large group of clocks which have survived the vicissitudes of age and experience only to fall into the hands of people who have altered and 'improved' them, sometimes to make them more fashionable and valuable. In this category must be counted those movements that have had new cases made for them which have been aged up to simulate the originals. Then, too, there are clocks which have had perfectly legitimate replacement cases made for them so long ago that now they could be mistaken for the originals. Finally, there are clocks which, purely for expediency, have been fitted into spare cases of other periods or have been fitted into later cases because their owners wished to update their appearance. More will be said about clocks that fall into these categories but first normal restoration will be discussed.

There is no doubt in the writer's mind that the best restoration work is that carried out under the aegis of a responsible dealer. Such a person will have handled many similar clocks before and, most important, will entrust each part of the work to the right specialist. He will ensure that any replacements are in keeping with the rest of the clock and are correct representations of what was missing. A responsible dealer has every interest in right restoration. If the clock is intended for his showroom then he will want it to look its best and perform well. If he is restoring a client's clock the same criteria will apply.

There is a world of difference between sensible, sympathetic restoration work, which involves putting back any missing parts and replacing with correct parts any previous bad repairs, and faking, which involves radically changing the original structure in order that the clock should finish up possessing features which make it more valuable but which it did not possess when it originally left the maker's workshop.

The clock illustrated by Isaac Rogers in Plate VII/1 is a good example of a clock that required sympathetic restoration. It will be seen that the case is of well-figured mahogany and is complete, though one or two joints needed tightening and gluing. The surface of the wood needed to be gently cleaned and waxed. The frets, feet and brass ornamentation were complete but all the brass work needed removing, polishing and re-lacquering against future tarnish. The silk behind the brass side frets of old clocks is almost invariably damaged or discoloured and it is customary to replace it with new silk of an appropriate tone and type.

Isaac Rogers' clock is desirably small, about 15½ inches tall, and is visibly a high class production. The brass-bound three pad top is a sought-after feature, as is a brass dial plate fitted with an enamel hour plate and subsidiaries. There is a rise and fall regulation feature, which allows the clock to be regulated without turning it round and adjusting the pendulum bob. Adjusting the pendulum bob to the right length for optimum timekeeping is no great hardship and, once adjusted, the timekeeping is unlikely to vary by an appreciable amount. Rise and fall mechanism from the front involves levers and cams and is thus more expensive. The dial is fitted with the usual strike/silent feature. The hands are original and of polished and lacquered brass. It is not apparent from the photograph, but the dial enamels were slightly chipped and discoloured. They were entrusted to a specialist ceramic restorer for cleaning and repair. The brass dial plate, which has engraved corners, needed polishing and re-lacquering, as did the hands.

The reverse view of Isaac Rogers' clock, Plate VII/2, shows that the movement has suffered from a typical Victorian or Edwardian overhaul. The original verge and contrate wheel had been removed and an anchor escapement put in their place. Fortunately the original backcock was retained. The bell strike had been replaced with a gong, a great Victorian favourite. For some unexplained reason the rise and fall mechanism had been removed.

The normal restoration procedure for a good antique bracket clock involves completely dismantling the movement. All the brass and steel work, including the pivots, is cleaned and polished. The pivot holes are bushed as necessary and the hands, if of steel, are re-blued after repairing and replacing if this is

PLATE VII/1 *Isaac Rogers.*
Mahogany three pad top clock.
Enamel dial plates fitted to an
engraved brass dial plate.
Before restoration.
Circa *1790.*

necessary. The dial plate and fittings will be polished and lacquered and the chapter ring and any other formerly silvered parts re-silvered and lacquered. A single sheet brass dial will be re-silvered and lacquered. Any repair work necessary will be performed and new gut or soft wire lines will be fitted to clocks not fitted with chain fusées. Finally, the movement will be re-assembled, oiled and adjusted before being put on test. This work requires many years of training and experience and should never be entrusted to an amateur enthusiast or attempted by the amateur.

Plate VII/3 shows Isaac Rogers' movement after cleaning and restoration. A suitable bell was procured and a hammer made and fitted. The rise and fall mechanism of a similar clock of the period, *circa* 1790, was used as a model for the replacement of the rise and fall mechanism. Brass of the same colour tone as the movement was used. The escapement has been put back to verge and a pendulum holdfast of the right 'fall down' style fitted to the existing holes. The clock is now very much as it left the maker's workshop and ready for many more years of service.

PLATE VII/2 *Rear view of Isaac Rogers' clock, showing Victorian conversion to anchor escapement and gong strike. Rise and fall mechanism removed.*

It should be mentioned that some people opine that a clock that has been converted from verge to anchor should be left in that state; the conversion being part of the clock's history. This is a specious argument. If a clock originally had a verge escapement that needed repair then it should have been repaired. In the unlikely case that it was beyond repair it should have been replaced with an identical verge escapement. Many earlier Georgian bracket clocks, and for that matter their predecessors, have not only been converted to anchor escapement but have also lost the pull-quarter repeating work that was such a popular feature of many expensive bracket clocks of the early Georgian period and before. If a repeat train and the associated mechanism is missing the new train must be made to the correct design using the original pivot holes.

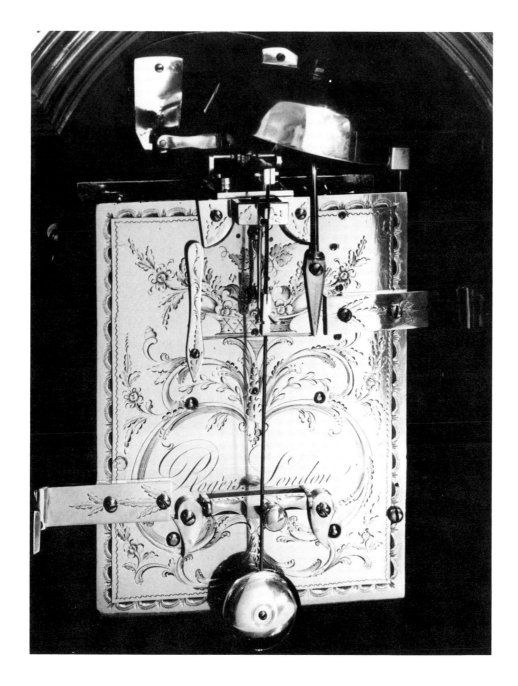

Legitimate restoration of a case will involve repairing or replacing any damaged or missing mouldings, frets and finials. It is always better to repair rather than replace but if, for example, one brass finial was missing a replacement should be cast using an existing finial as a pattern. The replacement should be cast in brass of the correct colour. The cabinetmaker will gently clean, 'revive', the original surface of the case and wax polish it. If the surface of the wood will not respond to this treatment because the original polished surface has completely deteriorated then he will strip, recolour and repolish it. All brass parts will be removed, polished, re-lacquered and refitted. Locks and hinges will be repaired as necessary.

Restoration work of the nature described certainly does not detract from the value of a clock if the work is carried out correctly and sympathetically. The

PLATE VII/4 *Thomas Colley. Believed to have been originally a black clock, now re-veneered with burr walnut or yew. Original mounts and dial retained but movement drastically altered.* Circa *1755.*

PLATE VII/5 *Clock signed John Baker, London. Possibly an altered or replaced dial.*

appearance of the clock will be considerably enhanced. But obviously a clock whose movement and case are entirely original will have the edge on it. Such clocks are extremely rare, even more so among the earlier examples. Good and correct restoration work will be declared by a reputable dealer. Indeed he will be proud of the fact the he has brought back life and the original appearance to a clock that was shabby, broken and a credit to nobody.

Plate VII/4 shows a clock of extremely attractive appearance with a case described to the writer as burr yew, or possibly walnut. The maker is Thomas Colley who, as he proclaims on the dial plate, was successor to George Graham. Thomas Colley had worked for Graham.

Thomas Colley's clock was probably made *circa* 1755. It stands 15½ inches high and, as one might expect, exhibits many features associated with Tompion and Graham. The handle and its pommels and the case mounts are exactly what one would expect. The backplate is plain, as is sometimes the case with Graham's clocks, but what would not show in a photograph is the large number of filled holes where repeating levers and mechanism of the type favoured by Tompion and Graham were once fitted. In fact the original repeating mechanism has been entirely removed and the clock has been made into a clock that quarter chimes on six bells with the hour being struck on a seventh bell. There is also no doubt in the writer's opinion that the clock case has been re-veneered, having started life as a black clock. This is a good example of a clock that has been drastically altered and, even though the work has been carried out extremely well, the clock would no longer be of particular interest to a discriminating collector. Nor in this instance would it be worthwhile to restore the clock correctly. So much has been changed that the amount of new restoration work would outweigh what remains of the original clock by far too great a degree. Clocks like this are sometimes described in the antique trade as furnishing pieces.

Plate VII/5 shows a dial plate that in the writer's opinion looks as if it may have been replaced or altered. The spandrels are too small for the dial and are of a pattern that was popular *circa* 1730. The hands are of crude appearance and are presumably modern. The design of the strike/silent ring and chapter ring is heavy and the whole layout of the dial looks wrong. The clock is signed 'John Baker London'. The signature is repeated on the backplate. The case gives every appearance of being early nineteenth century.

Two more examples of clocks remembered by the writer may be of interest. The first was a walnut inverted bell-top bracket clock apparently made *circa* 1740 by a London maker. In the opinion of a senior staff member of the auction house which sold the clock it had been completely re-veneered years earlier. He had formed his opinion after observing the overall evenness and depth of colour and pattern of the veneer. More faded parts would have been expected and a greater variation in surface texture. The moulding round the inside of the front door appeared very crisp and there were fewer old dents, knocks and repairs and fewer signs of shrinkage of the cross-grained mouldings than he would have expected in a clock of this age. The general feel and

PLATE VII/6 *The perils of owning a cat! A good late eighteenth century bracket clock by Alex Wilson after being knocked onto a stone floor by a cat.*

PLATE VII/7 *The Alex Wilson clock after skilful restoration.*

PLATE VII/8 *A gadroon top Regency case described as now containing a late seventeenth century pull-quarter repeating timepiece movement by John Rant.*

PLATE VII/9 *A three pad break-arch bracket clock case circa 1790 described as containing a late nineteenth century quarter chiming movement. Attached to an altered dial plate.*

PLATE VII/10 *A fine mahogany balloon clock described as being fitted with a good quality twentieth century movement. Percy Webster was a well-known dealer between the wars. The case possibly contemporary but could be late eighteenth century.*

PLATE VII/11 *Typical late eighteenth century ebonised case, but the maker, John Briggs, Skipton, is recorded in the nineteenth century. The spandrels of an early eighteenth or late seventeenth century pattern. The chapter ring in the style popular* circa *1745.*

appearance of the walnut of the case was certainly different to that evinced, for example, by the clock by Sanderson of Wigton shown in Colour Plate 2. But in the writer's opinion it was also perfectly possible that the case of this walnut clock had become very shabby and that at some time thirty or forty years ago it had been stripped, repaired and polished which could have accounted for its relatively pristine appearance.

The re-veneering of black clocks with walnut was discussed in Chapter II. The rule must be to examine all walnut bracket clocks extremely carefully. If there is any doubt about the originality of the veneer an expert opinion should be sought. A walnut clock that has been re-veneered or re-polished is less valuable than one that retains its original veneer and patination. It should be remembered that many ebony or ebonised Georgian clocks have brass mounts and brass fillets round their doors and sound apertures, thus making a fine contrast between the black of the case and the gold of the dial and mounts.

PLATE VII/12 *(left) Alexander Cummings. A fine eighteenth century musical movement described as being in an associated case. Note the added 'Tempus Fugit' to enable the movement to fit the fine replacement 'Chippendale' case.*

PLATE VII/13 *(above) Abraham Weston. Lewes. Unrestored black lacquer timepiece repeating clock in very untouched original condition. The same clock is shown after sympathetic restoration in Plate III/1.*

Walnut cases were usually, but not invariably, made without such brass fillets and mounts. Evidently and confusingly there are also a number of perfectly genuine walnut cases to which brass mounts and embellishments were added later.

The second clock recalled was a handsome break-arch bracket clock signed by a London maker working *circa* 1790. But the case had a dark heavy finish and large clumsy-looking sound apertures in the sides. The hinges too had a heavy Victorian appearance. The dial at first sight looked authentically late eighteenth century but a point noted was that the dial centre was not well matted but merely gave a rough cast appearance; could this have been a dial plate that was formerly painted? The movement and backplate gave every appearance of having been made about 1790.

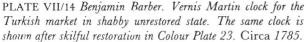

PLATE VII/14 *Benjamin Barber. Vernis Martin clock for the Turkish market in shabby unrestored state. The same clock is shown after skilful restoration in Colour Plate 23.* Circa *1785.*

PLATE VII/15 *Gibbs. An apparently unremarkable small rosewood quarter chiming bracket clock* circa *1830. Described as being fitted with an earlier movement. See Plate VII/16.*

Three possibilities occurred to us. First the clock was right and original save for that the case had been re-polished to that curious dark 'Victorian' colour and the hinges and locks replaced. The lack of fine matting in the dial centre could just be explained by the fact that it is possible to drastically overclean a dial and thus soften, or even lose, fine matting. The second possibility was that the clock had started life with a painted dial that had subsequently been converted into a mounted brass dial. A painted brass dial from which the paint had been removed would have a slightly rough surface, not unlike fine matting which has been softened. The third possibility was that the case was a replacement made much later than the movement and was, perhaps, even Edwardian. There must be many a movement which, its case having been lost or damaged beyond repair, has had a new case made for it in a style approximating to the original. Given another seventy or eighty years of handling, use and polishing it could be difficult to detect the change.

These discussions illustrate how difficult it can be to decide whether a clock is 'right' or wrong. But the point just raised about the alteration of dials merits further explanation. Georgian bracket clocks made towards the end of the eighteenth century or during the first thirty years of the nineteenth century were, if not made with dials mounted with chapter rings and spandrels, often fitted with single sheet brass dials which were engraved and silvered. Alternatively they were made with painted dials. Bracket clocks with painted dials by London or better provincial makers differed from contemporary longcase painted dials in that the white base paint was usually applied to a brass dial sheet rather than the iron sheet used for longcase dials. The writer believes that many shabby painted dial bracket clocks have been been 'improved' by removing the paint and then polishing the surface. The resultant smooth brass sheet can then be engraved and silvered to produce a silvered brass dial clock that as such is apparently more valuable than a clock with a painted dial. Such a change is extremely hard to detect. The back of the dial plate will give every appearance of being original. Indeed it is original. Equally, the overlapping period of manufacture will continue to allow the clock to be right for period.

Both original silvered brass dial and painted dial bracket clocks of this period are also ripe for conversion into clocks with brass dials mounted with chapter rings and spandrels. If the backplate is plain it is sometimes engraved. The verge escapement was fitted as original equipment to many early nineteenth century bracket clocks and would thus continue to look exactly right on a clock altered as just described. It should also be remembered that a skilled clockmaker would have no difficulty whatsoever in making a mounted brass dial plate or an engraved silvered single sheet brass dial. 'Suitable' examples have also been converted into clocks with brass dial plates and enamel hour and subsidiary dials. Such dials can then be aged up and fitted to the movements of his choice. No doubt there are some clocks that have had new dials fitted as genuine repairs but in such instances one would also expect to see evidence of extensive repair to the case.

A checklist in the form of a number of questions is offered which may be useful when examining a clock:

1. The maker. When and where was he working and do the features of the dial movement and case appear to be of that period?

2. Does the outside of the case look original, i.e. right veneer, right doors, right locks and hinges, right feet? Or has the case been damaged and badly repaired at some time or been altered? If it looks merely battered but unbowed are all the mouldings those you would expect for its period? The underside of the case should also be looked at, particularly if the clock is early Georgian. The inside of the case should also be examined. The foundation wood should be of old oak or possibly pine in the case of a lacquer clock. The parts that show were usually stained black in an ebonised or ebony veneered case but were usually left in the natural state in cases veneered with walnut or mahogany. Lacquer on pine cases were usually painted inside, often a pinkish red, probably to deter woodworm. The inside of a black case re-veneered with walnut may still be black or have a bleached appearance if the black has been removed. Later genuine replacement cases should be recognised as being later due to the fact that they will look newer. But it is not unknown for an exact and correct replica

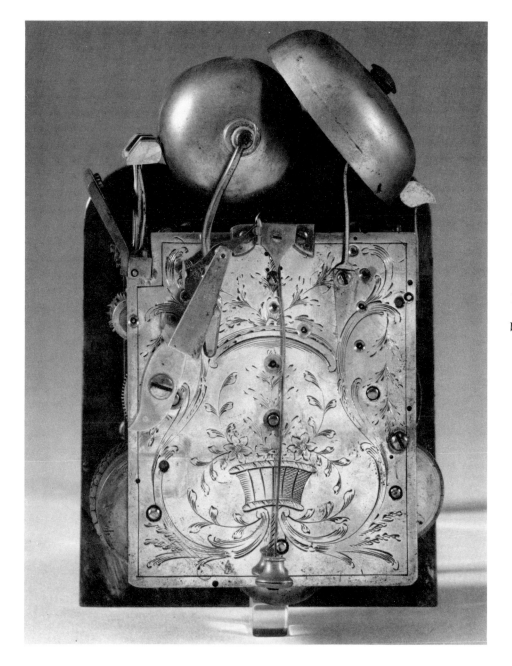

case to be made for a good movement that has lost its case and for the case to be deliberately aged up. The most recent example seen by the writer gave every appearance of being late seventeenth century, yet was less than three months old.

3. The dial. Does it fit the wooden mask surrounding it? Has the mask been completely replaced, as opposed to mended? Are the spandrels, hands, chapter ring, engraving and other applied parts of the period and design obtaining at the time? If a date ring is fitted, do the numerals have an engraving style consistent with those of the chapter ring? Are there signs of filled holes or inexplicable unfilled holes in the dial plate? If so, why? Do the winding squares protrude too far through the winding holes or lie too far back from them? Dials with automata or phases of the moon should be examined to see if these features are original or later additions.

PLATE VII/17 *Simon de Charmes. An eighteenth century walnut bracket clock described as having an altered movement and having been re-veneered.*

4. The movement and fittings. Does the dial plate fit the recess in which it lies behind the mask? With any fixing straps and bottom securing bolts properly tightened and fitted do the dial and movement fit the case and go together as you would expect? Allow for any apparent movement or shrinkage of the case. Are there any filled or unused holes in the rear side styles which might make you wonder if another movement was once fitted to the case? If rotating locking cams are fitted to the back of the dial plate, a feature often found on early Georgian clocks, check that there are corresponding grooves showing signs of use to take them in each front style. If there are holes in the bottom of the case, do they line up with corresponding threaded holes in the lower movement pillars, i.e. were there, or are there, fixing bolts through the bottom of the case? Holes which do not correspond with threaded movement pillar holes are not necessarily sinister. They may have been used to secure the clock to a wall bracket. Does the seatboard, if there is one, look original? Are there empty holes in either the front or the backplate of the movement? Do the dial feet look original and is the back of the dial of old, well-planished cast brass? The back of the dial and the movement plates should show some signs of wear and scratches occasioned by pins and screws being removed when the clock has been taken apart and re-assembled over the years. Equally, there should be evidence of re-bushing of pivots and wear in the pinions. The under dial work should also be checked for previous repairs and replacements and to ensure that the motion work, striking work and date drive are complete.

If the clock has a verge escapement has it always had it or has it been converted back? Look for filled holes and signs of alteration. Is the backcock original? Has the clock been converted to anchor? Do the wheels and collets look right for period? If the clock has, or looks as if it once had, repeating work check for holes in the movement and filled holes in the case which would have carried the repeat cord. A reason for filled movement holes should always be found; apart from those arising from original changes of plan by the maker or verge conversions or the removal of repeating trains. It is also not unknown for timepiece pull repeating clocks, i.e. clocks with a single fusée, to be converted into striking clocks with twin fusées. A striking clock is usually worth more than a timepiece of the same period by the same maker. There are also many clocks which have been re-trained by Victorian or Edwardian restorers who did not realise that it is best to repair existing trains. Finally, is there any possibility that the clock is a turn of the twentieth century, or even later, reproduction of an earlier nineteenth century clock that has been aged up and had an earlier name repainted on the painted or enamel dial?

The questions put in the foregoing questionnaire will be easily understood by the intelligent amateur enthusiast but he or she may not always know or understand the answers to them. The most experienced dealer too will readily admit that from time to time he encounters features in a clock that puzzle him. Yet it must also be apparent that a good dealer will have examined more clocks in a year than the amateur, who must of necessity spend his working day in some other employment, will see in his lifetime. A dealer has another advantage. Over the years he will have had the chance to see and handle many examples of the work of different makers. He will know what to expect in a clock by a particular maker and he will know what differences to expect between the movements and cases of the different periods. He is constantly adding to an ever increasing fund of knowledge and experience. He will also acquire considerable knowledge and experience of restoration work.

It is believed that most really good collections, be they clocks, pictures, or furniture, have been built up by collectors who have made an ally of and worked in conjunction with a good and knowledgeable dealer in that field.

A sensible way of making a good purchase is to visit a number of dealers in order to gain some idea of the sort of clocks in which each of them deals. Most people will also be able to form a judgement about the dealer himself and his *modus operandi*. If a clock is seen at an auction or is offered privately it is always best to ask a good dealer to give an opinion and bid or act for you. You must pay him his fee, but it will be worth it.

It is, in the writer's view, unwise to bid at auction without having had the benefit of a good dealer's opinion. Auctioneers act merely as agents for the vendor and most catalogues point out that the auctioneers accept no responsibility for errors or omissions of description. To bid at auction without considerable knowledge and experience can be disappointing and expensive. The writer has on more than one occasion seen private individuals buy what they imagined to be great bargains at auction, yet nearly every time the so-called bargain was sold cheaply because the experienced dealers present were not

PLATE VII/18 *John Bushman. A second (see Plate I/13) example of a small ebonised chiming clock in a very early bell-top case.* Circa *1710.*

bidding, knowing there was something wrong with the clock in question. Some words from John Ruskin are not out of place:

> 'It's unwise to pay too much...but it's worse to pay too little. When you pay too much you loose a little money... that is all. When you pay too little, you sometimes lose everything because the thing you bought was incapable of doing the thing it was bought to do. The common law of business balance prohibits paying a little and getting a lot...it can't be done. If you deal with the lowest bidder, it is as well to add something for the risk you run. And if you do that, you will have enough to pay for something better.'

A final point. Often when something very unusual appears it is dismissed as being wrong. The clock illustrated in Plate I/13 was at first excluded from this book because the writer had never seen anything quite like it and concluded that the apparently very early true bell-top of the case was a later replacement. Long after the manuscript had been completed a virtually identically cased clock by the same maker was offered for sale (Plate VII/18). It seems likely that both these very attractive small clocks are exactly as they appear, i.e. in their original unaltered cases. But as all collectors know, the discovery of something rare and unusual is one of the great pleasures of collecting.

Photographic Acknowledgements

Photographs are identified by Colour Plate numbers or Chapter/Plate numbers. The photographs used were chosen from a very large selection. My thanks to those who provided them and to those kind people who provided photographs which could not be included.

Asprey PLC. I/7, II/10, II/43, III/3, IV/3, IV/14, IV/17, IV/19, IV/42, IV/76, IV/94, IV/96, IV/97, V/7, V/13, V/16, VI/11, VI/17, VI/24, VI/35, VI/51, VI/53. Colour Plates 2, 3, 12, 13, 14, 23, 25, 26, 28, 30.

Richard Barder Antiques. I/1, I/2, I/3, I/4, I/5, I/8, II/2, II/3, II/4, II/5, II/7, II/8, II/9, II/12, II/13, II/14, II/15, II/16, II/38, II/39, II/54, III/1, IV/9, IV/23. IV/27, IV/28, IV/29, IV/35, IV/36, IV/37, IV/38, IV/41, IV/44, IV/45, IV/46, IV/59, IV/60, IV/62. IV/63, IV/66, IV/70, IV/77, IV/78, IV/79, IV/80, IV/81, IV/82, IV/83, IV/85, IV/88, IV/89, IV.91, VI/1, VI/2, VI/3, VI/4, VI/6, VI/7. VI/15, VI/16, VI/26, VI/39, VI/40, VI/41, VI/42, VI/43, VI/50, VII/1, VII/2, VII/3, VII/6, VII/7. Colour Plates 5, 7, 8.

Bonham's Ltd. VI/33.

British Museum. (Trustees of the British Museum.) I/9, II/19, II/20, II/21, IV/99, IV/100, IV/101, IV/102, IV/103.

Christie's. II/22, II/23, II/24, II/25, II/34, II/45, II/46, II/49, II/51, II/52, III/2, IV/11, IV/39, IV/40, IV/52, IV/75, IV/98, V/3, V/6, V/8, V/10, VI/12, VI/19, VI/22, VI/25, VII/14, VII/15, VII/16. Colour Plates. 1, 4, 15, 19, 21.

P.G. Dawson. I/12, IV/1, IV/10, IV/16, IV/68, IV/92, V/1, V/9, VI/45.

Evans and Evans. IV/25, IV/47, IV/48, IV/67, IV/93, VI/9, VI/23.

Good Hope Antiques. IV/37.

Holloway's. V/4. Colour Plate 16.

Lalonde Brothers, & Parham Ltd. III/4.

Ronald A. Lee. (Fine Arts.) Ltd. I/5, I/6, II/28, II/33, IV/2, IV/6, IV/13, IV/15. Colour Plate 6.

Brian Loomes. I/11, IV/49, IV/50, IV/51.

Mallett. II/31, III/6, III/7, V/4, V/15. Colour Plates 10, 24.

Neale's. VII/7.

P. and M. Oxley. IV/21, IV/22, IV/55, IV/56, IV/57.

Phillip's Son and Neale Ltd. II/57, IV/20, IV/53, IV/95, V/12, VI/5, VI/31, VI/38, VII/9, VII/17

D. and S. Pullen. IV/28. Colour Plate 31.

Raffety. II/32, II/33.

Sotheby's. Frontispiece, I/10, I/13, II/6, II/17, II/18, II/36, II/37, II/40, II/50, II/53, II/55, II/56, III/5, III/8, IV/7, IV/8, IV/12, IV/18, IV/21, IV/24, IV/26, IV/30, IV/31, IV/32, IV/33, IV/34, IV/43, IV/54, IV/61, IV/64, IV/65, IV/69, IV/71, IV/84, IV/86, IV/87, IV/90, V/2. V/14, VI/8, VI/10, VI/13, VI/14, VI/18, VI/20, VI/21, VI/34, VI/36, VI/44, VI/47, VI/49, VI/52, VII/5, VII/10, VII/11, VII/12, VII/13. Colour Plates. 9, 11, 17, 18, 20, 22, 27, 29.

Henry Spencer. Retford. II/11.

Strike One (Islington) Ltd. II/41, II/42, VI/27, VI/32, VI/48.

Victoria and Albert Museum. (Trustees of the Victoria and Albert Museum.) II/1, II/29, II/30, II/44, II/47, II/48, IV/58, V/5, V/11.

Anthony Woodburn Ltd. II/26, II/27, IV/4, IV/5, IV/72, IV/73, VI/46.

Woolley and Wallis. IV/74, VI/29, VII/18.

List of Colour Plates

Note: All clock colour plate and black and white captions describe London-made clocks unless otherwise indicated.

Bibliography

Bibliography. Including authorities referred to in the text and footnotes.

Atkins, C.E, *Register of Apprentices of the Worshipful Company of Clockmakers of the City of London*, privately printed, 1931.

Baillie, G.H., *Watchmakers and Clockmakers of the World*. First edn. Methuen & Co. Ltd., London, 1929. Reprinted as Vol. 1, N.A.G. Press, London, 1976.

Baillie, G.H., Clutton, C., Ilbert, C.A., *Britten's Old Clocks and Watches and their Makers*, 9th edn., Methuen in association with E. & F.N. Spon, London, 1982.

Barder, R.C.R., *English Country Grandfather Clocks. The Brass-Dial Longcase*, David & Charles, Newton Abbott, 1983.

Barker, D., *The Arthur Negus Guide to English Clocks*, Hamlyn, London 1980.

Beeson, C.F.C., *Clockmaking in Oxfordshire*, Museum of the History of Science, Oxford, 1967.

Bellchambers, J.K., *Somerset Clockmakers*, Antiquarian Horological Society, 1968; *Devonshire Clockmakers*, The Devonshire Press, Torquay, 1962.

Bentley, W.J., *The Plain Man's Guide to Antique Clocks*, Michael Joseph, London, 1963.

Bird, A., *English House Clocks, 1600-1850*, David & Charles, Newton Abbot, 1973.

Britten, F.J., *Old English Clocks, The Wetherfield Collection*. First pub. Lawrence & Jellicoe, London, 1907. New edn. Antique Collectors' Club, Woodbridge, 1980; *Old Clocks and Watches and their Makers*, first edn. Batsford, London, 1898. Antique Collectors' Club, Woodbridge, 1977.

Brown, H. Miles, *Cornish Clocks and Clockmakers*, David & Charles, Newton Abbot, 1961.

Bruton, E., *Clocks and Watches*, Hamlyn, London, 1968; *The Wetherfield Collection of Clocks. A guide to dating English Antique Clocks*, N.A.G. Press, London, 1981.

Butler, R, *The Arthur Negus Guide to English Furniture*, Hamlyn, London, 1978.

De Carle, D., *Clocks and their Value*, N.A.G. Press, London, 1968.

Cescinsky, H. and Webster, M., *English Domestic Clocks*. First pub. George Routledge and Sons, London, 1913. Reproduced Hamlyn, London, 1969.

Cumhaill, P.W., *Investing in Clocks and Watches*, Barrie and Rockliff, London, 1967.

Daniels, G., *Freemen of the Worshipful Company of Clockmakers, 1631-1984*, Daniels, 1984.

Dawson, P.G., *The Iden Clock Collection*, Antique Collectors' Club, Woodbridge, 1987.

Dawson, P.G., Drover, C.B., Parkes, D.W., *Early English Clocks*, Antique Collectors' Club, Woodbridge, 1982.

Dowler, G., *Gloucestershire Clocks and Watchmakers*, Phillimore, London, 1984.

Elliot, D.J., *Shropshire Clocks and Clockmakers*, Phillimore, London, 1979.

Haggar, A.L., Miller, L.F., *Suffolk Clocks and Clockmakers*, Antiquarian Horological Society, 1974.

Hayden, A., *Chats on Old Clocks*, Fisher Unwin, London, 1917.

Hobson, C., Harvey, L., Allix, C., *Hobson's Choice*, Malcolm Gardner, Sevenoaks, 1982.

Jagger, C., *Clocks*, Orbis, London, 1973; *Royal Clocks*, Robert Hale, London, 1983; *The World's Great Clocks and Watches*, Hamlyn, London, 1977.

Joy, E.T., *Country Life Book of Clocks*, Hamlyn, London, 1967; *English Furniture. 1800-1851*, Sotheby Parke Bernet, Ward Lock, London, 1977.

Kurz, O., *European Clocks and Watches in the Near East*, Warburg Inst., University of London, 1975. E.J. Brill, Leiden.

Bibliography

Lee, R.A., *The Knibb Family. Clockmakers*, Manor House Press, Byfleet, 1964.

Lloyd, H.A., *Chats on Old Clocks*, Ernest Benn, London, 1951; *Old Clocks*, Benn, 1951; *Some Outstanding Clocks over 700 Years*, Leonard Hill, London, 1958; *Collectors' Dictionary of Clocks*. Hamlyn, 1964.

Loomes, B., *Country Clocks and their London Origins*, David & Charles, Newton Abbot, 1976; *Watchmakers and Clockmakers of the World*, Vol. 2, N.A.G. Press, London, 1976; *Complete British Clocks*, David & Charles, 1978; *The Early Clockmakers of Great Britain*, N.A.G. Press, London, 1981; *White Dial Clocks*, David & Charles, 1981.

Maitzner, F., Moreau, J., *La Comtoise, La Morbier, La Morez*, France, 1979.

Mason, B., *Clock and Watchmakers in Colchester*, Hamlyn, London, 1969.

Nicholls, A., *English Bracket and Mantel clocks*, Blandford, Poole, 1981.

Pearson, M., *The Beauty of Clocks*, Colour Library International, New Malden, 1979.

Penfold, J.B., *The Clockmakers of Cumberland*, Brant Wright Associates, Ashford, 1977.

Ponsford, C.N., *Time in Exeter*, Headwell Vale Books, Exeter, 1978; *Devonshire Clocks and Clockmakers*, David & Charles, Newton Abbot, 1985.

Price, B., *The Story of English Furniture*, BBC, London, 1978.

Pryce, W.T.R., Davies, T.A., *Samuel Roberts. Clockmaker*, National Museum of Wales, 1985.

Roberts, Deryck, *The Bracket Clock*, David & Charles, Newton Abbot, 1982.

Robinson, T.O., *The Longcase Clock*, Antique Collectors' Club, Woodbridge, 1978.

Rose, R.E., *English Dial Clocks*, Antique Collectors' Club, Woodbridge, 1978.

Smith, A., *Clocks and Watches*, The Connoisseur, London, 1975; *The Country Life International Dictionary of Clocks*, Hamlyn, London, 1979.

Smith, John, *Old Scottish Clockmakers*, Oliver and Boyd, London, 1921.

Symonds, R.W., *Masterpieces of English Furniture and Clocks*, B.T. Batsford, London, 1940; *Thomas Tompion, His Life and Work,* B.T. Batsford, London, 1951.

Tribe, T., Whatmoor, P., *Dorset Clocks and Clockmakers*, Tanet Books, Oswestry, 1981.

Tyler, E.J., *The Clockmakers of Sussex*, The Watch and Clock Book Society, Ashford.

White, Sir George, *English Lantern Clocks*, Antique Collectors' Club, Woodbridge, 1989.

White, Lady Elizabeth (Compiler), *Pictorial Dictionary of British 18th Century Furniture Design. The printed sources*, Antique Collectors' Club, Woodbridge, 1990.

Ullyett, K., *In Quest of Clocks*, Barrie and Rockliff, London, 1950; *British Clocks and Clockmakers*, Collins, London, 1957.

Makers' Index

Index

Index

The Antique Collectors' Club

The Antique Collectors' Club was formed in 1966 and now has a five figure membership spread throughout the world. It publishes the only independently run monthly antiques magazine *Antique Collecting* which caters for those collectors who are interested in widening their knowledge of antiques, both by greater awareness of quality and by discussion of the factors which influence the price that is likely to be asked. The Antique Collectors' Club pioneered the provision of information on prices for collectors and the magazine still leads in the provision of detailed articles on a variety of subjects.

It was in response to the enormous demand for information on 'what to pay' that the price guide series was introduced in 1968 with the first edition of *The Price Guide to Antique Furniture* (completely revised, 1978 and 1989), a book which broke new ground by illustrating the more common types of antique furniture, the sort that collectors could buy in shops and at auctions rather than the rare museum pieces which had previously been used (and still to a large extent are used) to make up the limited amount of illustrations in books published by commercial publishers. Many other price guides have followed, all copiously illustrated, and greatly appreciated by collectors for the valuable information they contain, quite apart from prices. The Antique Collectors' Club also publishes other books on antiques, including horology and art reference works, and a full book list is available.

Club membership, which is open to all collectors, costs £19.50 per annum. Members receive free of charge *Antique Collecting,* the Club's magazine (published ten times a year), which contains well-illustrated articles dealing with the practical aspects of collecting not normally dealt with by magazines. Prices, features of value, investment potential, fakes and forgeries are all given prominence in the magazine.

Among other facilities available to members are private buying and selling facilities, the longest list of 'For Sales' of any antiques magazine, an annual ceramics conference and the opportunity to meet other collectors at their local antique collectors' clubs. There are over eighty in Britain and more than a dozen overseas. Members may also buy the Club's publications at special pre-publication prices.

As its motto implies, the Club is an organisation designed to help collectors get the most out of their hobby: it is informal and friendly and gives enormous enjoyment to all concerned.

For Collectors — By Collectors — About Collecting

The Antique Collectors' Club, 5 Church Street, Woodbridge, Suffolk